DISTURB /
ENRAPTURE

SIBLING RIVALRY PRESS is an independent press based in Little Rock, Arkansas, with a mission to publish work that disturbs and enraptures, like the journal you are reading right now. It is a sponsored project of Fractured Atlas, a nonprofit arts service organization. Contributions to support the operations of Sibling Rivalry Press are tax-deductible to the extent permitted by law, and your donations will directly assist in the publication of work that disturbs and enraptures. To contribute to the publication of more projects like this one, please visit our website and click donate. Help us build bridges and save lives.

WWW.SIBLINGRIVALRYPRESS.COM

ASSARACUS
A JOURNAL OF GAY AND QUEER POETRY

28

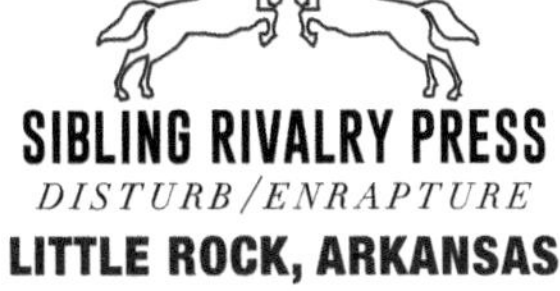

SIBLING RIVALRY PRESS
DISTURB/ENRAPTURE
LITTLE ROCK, ARKANSAS

Cover image: "Wigstock in Tompkins Square, East Village"
by Efrain John Gonzalez. Used with permission.

Sibling Rivalry Press
159 Sunset Drive
North Little Rock, AR 72118
info@siblingrivalrypress.com
www.siblingrivalrypress.com

Printed in the United States of America.

Bryan Borland is founding publisher of Sibling Rivalry Press and founding editor of *Assaracus: A Journal of Gay and Queer Poetry*. His most recent books include *Brotherful*, a finalist for the Publishing Triangle's Thom Gunn Award for Gay Poetry, and the chapbook *Crow in the Desert*. Previous titles include the chapbook *Tourist* (2018), and three full-length collections of poems: *My Life as Adam* (2010), *Less Fortunate Pirates: Poems from the First Year Without My Father* (2012), and *DIG* (2016), which was a finalist for the Lambda Literary Award in Gay Poetry and a Stonewall Honor Book in Literature as selected by the American Library Association. He is a Windgate Foundation Catalyze Fellow, a Lambda Literary Fellow in Poetry, and a winner of the Judith A. Markowitz Emerging Writer Award from the Lambda Literary Foundation.

www.bryanborland.com

ISBN: 978-1-943977-95-6
ISSN: 2159-0478

Assaracus Issue 28: A Journal of Gay and Queer Poetry
April 2026.

IF YOU ARE NOT QUEER
QUEER POETRY
IS NOT YOUR
SAFE SPACE.
YOU ARE WELCOME
BUT YOUR COMFORT
IS NOT OUR PRIORITY.

OUR JOY IS.
OUR SEX IS.
OUR ART IS.
OUR LIVES ARE.
OUR SURVIVAL IS.

COVER PHOTOGRAPH

WIGSTOCK IN TOMPKINS SQUARE, EAST VILLAGE

EFRAIN JOHN GONZALEZ

THE PHOTOGRAPHS OF EFRAIN JOHN GONZALEZ HAVE BEEN INCLUDED IN MUSEUM EXHIBITIONS, REPRODUCED IN SCHOLARLY PUBLICATIONS, AND FEATURED IN NUMEROUS SOLO GALLERY SHOWS. GONZALEZ HAS BEEN DOCUMENTING ALMOST EVERY ASPECT OF THE QUEER COMMUNITY FOR OVER FOUR DECADES.

SUPPORT QUEER ARTISTS.
FOR MORE = **WWW.HELLFIREPRESS.COM**

FEATURING

LOVES OF MY LIFE

BOOK: If you've never read Audre Lorde's *Zami: A New Spelling of My Name: A Biomythography (Penguin Vitae)*, trust me on this. Stop what you're doing, call your local indie bookstore, and have them order you a copy of the beautiful new edition. Allow me to quote an early paragraph and imagine your bodies writhing in literary pleasure, dear/queer readers. I can't do it better than this:

> *To whom do I owe the woman I have become?*
>
> DeLois lived up the block on 142nd Street and never had her hair done, and all the neighborhood women sucked their teeth as she walked by. Her crispy hair twinkled in the summer sun as her big proud stomach moved her on down the block while I watched, not caring whether or not she was a poem. Even though I tied my shoes and tried to peep under her blouse as she passed by, I never spoke to DeLois, because my mother didn't. But I loved her, because she moved like she felt she was somebody special, like she was somebody I'd like to know someday. She moved like how I thought god's mother must have moved, and my mother, once upon a time, and someday maybe me.

NAMES: Speaking of love, those of you with astute eyes will notice the editor's husband, Seth, shifting to write as S.A. Borland. In fact, his first published poem under that name appears in this issue thanks to guest curator Jeff Walt. And speaking of names, shout out to Jeff, Jason, and Megan for making guest appearances in my poem at the end of this issue.

MORE BOOKS & POETS: Jeffery Berg was featured in Issue 10 of *Assaracus*, and he and publisher Indolent Books were kind enough to send me an early copy of his forthcoming *Re-Animator*. Berg proves himself a poet of memory and mischief, of camp and catastrophe, of heart. These poems remind me that the things I once thought disposable, like the B-movies, the overplayed pop songs, the awkward boyhood moments, are often what *build* us. This collection is strange, dazzling, and alive.

SRP's first official toe back in the publishing pool is the chapbook *Trillion Amber Trumpets* by JC Andrews, which I am including as part of the Arkansas Queer Poet Series. JC's book is weather and family and lust and dirt, all the things that make Arkansas special to me. Mark my words and remember her name. JC Andrews is the real deal.

XOXO // BB

SEAN BUGG

SAFEWORDS AS REPLACEMENTS FOR PRAYER

SEAN BUGG IS A POET WHO USED TO LIVE IN RICHMOND, VIRGINIA, BUT WHO NOW LIVES IN THE MIDWEST WHERE HE'S INCREASINGLY FASCINATED BY ITS LIMINAL SPACES: FIELDS, HIGHWAY UNDERPASSES, AND COURT SQUARES. HE WRITES ABOUT WHAT HE FINDS INESCAPABLE—DESIRE, THE DIVINE, AND DICK—FRAMED AGAINST, AND INSPIRED BY, THE INTERSECTION OF POETRY, CINEMA, AND PHOTOGRAPHY. HE'S PARTICULARLY INTERESTED IN FILMING AND DOCUMENTING THE "SUPPOSEDLY" UNFILMABLE—ESPECIALLY SPACES AND EXPERIENCES LARGELY CONSIDERED "IMPOLITE." FOR MORE OF HIS WORK, CHECK OUT *VOLUME POETRY* **("STAGE DIRECTIONS") AND** *NEW RIVER JOURNAL***. HE'S CURRENTLY ENROLLED IN THE MFA PROGRAM AT INDIANA UNIVERSITY—BLOOMINGTON.**

DARKROOM EPISTLE

Do you forget what night returns to us?
Perfume-clogged air? Sharp swells of strange
bodies: their backs pressed against walls?
Like all things in this temple of disco
& lights, he smells like patchouli & musk
mixed with leather: & tastes like stale tobacco
from his mouth to his hips. Normally, you
would balk at being bossed this way: but you
know if you goad him you'll get exactly
what you want: by which you mean the rough
luxury of his voice as it crashes into you
as he pins your arms: & cuffs them above
your head. Last week the word Sir was foreign:
something sterile, spoken only to elders.
This week you watch him slip you into
one cage after another: soft clicks: him
not knowing you like it when you're forced
into ugly choices by men who choose
safewords as replacements for prayer. He
says: *Like that*. He says: *My boy, you will not*
find the God you seek here. He says: *my dear*
I want you to beg.

NEON SIGNS ARE ONLY APPROPRIATE FOR SEX SHOPS & TAKE-OUT COUNTERS

Of him, you ask only the grammar of accident:
a couch: a popcorn bowl: a blanket: two hands:
a better-than-average horror film: you ask only
a slant of want, & get mixed signals: a constant
need for approval. Don't get it wrong you stan
a man adept at the art of self-deprecation: a man
who's hot but doesn't know it: a man who paints
his nails & lifts: someone with star-bright eyes &
cornsilk hair. The fuck did cornsilk come from?
Clearly you've been in Indiana too long already.
But fuck if Zoë didn't tell you ages ago, after the
gumbo fiasco: after you stopped her from taking
out her hoops: after she'd already filed down her
nails to points, he wasn't worth it: & damn if Ash
only needs an hour's notice & points before she's
ready to bury a body in the desert. Which one? It
doesn't matter: she just needs to call the sitter b/c
her husband is on business: & damned if Lola like
a sage doesn't tell you: *Sean, try as you may, you*
can't push the river: & damned if that doesn't re-
mind you of the Emperor in *Mulan*: a movie you
tolerate despite its casual racism & many historic
inaccuracies because it's got bomb-ass music: &
fuck if Kathleen doesn't agree there's no universe
in which *just friends* send endless shirtless selfies
over Snapchat: just like there's not a world where
you don't recognize the complexion of his soul:
or how his voice has been stained by grief. Thank
whatever god you believe in you didn't send him
that letter you wrote: that you didn't decide to stay
the night he drank too much: when he all but beg-
ged you. Thank whatever god comes next he didn't
come closer that night you made him dinner & he
had the audacity to look over his shoulder & say:

You're a messy cook. & thank whichever deity is leftover for the damn-near 800 mi. between y'all now because you know he would ruin you if only to prove a point.

INSTAGRAM THIRST TRAPS ARE THE ONLY REASON THIS POEM EXISTS

It's not even noon: & you've already confessed
to Marlee how quickly you'd get down on your
knees if ever you were given the chance to meet
him: Yungblud: in fact the exact words she used
were: *it's not even noon*: *we need to calm down*:
& you freely admit you lost it the minute he put
the microphone in his pants: to which she claps-
back: *baby what mic*: this man makes you want
to sin right there in public: this man makes you
want to commit un-speakable acts just to prove:
you can: this man knows just how to turn up his
lips in a way that drops panties straight through
the Earth to China: & again Marlee with the: *no*
NOT CHINA: this man his eyes betray someone
who knows how to find their way with a tongue
through the dark: Christ even Satan himself can't
smolder like that: where does he get the audacity?
So what if you've got a type: so what if it's bad-
boys with dark auras who are: give-or-take: just
a foot taller than you? So what if that type comes
mostly from the UK: or Europe at large? And so
what if it started with the random blond-boy out-
side the London airport in 2009: the one wearing
a trench-coat in mid-July: the one with the rock-
star hair who asked you for a light after clearing
customs? So what if you left the country instead
of cramming for finals just to cram yourself into
bathroom stalls with men you've only just met?
Under normal conditions you wouldn't wait this
long to mention God: but you're one obsession
away from becoming her weapon. How's that
for extravagance?

TRIPTYCH IN 5 PARTS AT THE NAIL SALON

1.

Maybe it's the spectacle of it all, of picking
out color like a child picks out green M&Ms
because they're the only ones worth saving
& taste the best: or is it maybe you like their
eyes so neatly rounded casting lines as if to
say *is he, you know*: or maybe it's the down-
right thrill of making them wonder whether
your belt is a bit loose that keeps you coming
back:

2.

At least this mother doesn't seem as awful
as the others: at least she has a nose ring &
hair that doesn't make you wonder whether
she knows what product is: at least she doesn't
wear Rocawear knock-offs: this mother
has an ass that says *I too know the exact type*
of delicate required to pump heels the way
you do:

3.

What if they knew that despite your browser
search history, you don't actually enjoy people
touching your feet : what if instead you stood
on each of your crash outs: what if excluding
this stranger whose hands descale your skin,
they knew you'd only been touched twice in
the past six months by other people: & not a
damn one of them left you debilitated. What
more must a boy do to feel exquisite?

4.

Consider this: the Romans had more words
to describe a twink than they did for war—
Mollis may be your favorite for no reason
other than: most commonly used in tempering
toxic masculinity into something more quietly
pleasing: like an unrealized riot: like a silent
rave: which is no place for someone: soft as
you.

5.

It happened once your father took you out to
the woods: a deer blind which also was made
of wood: that was your first taste of cold iron
& steel on the tongue: but it wouldn't be your
last: his hand when he made you hold a gun:
his hands not painted like these: hands which
still sifted just fine: gunpowder between flask
& barrel. *Please excuse the mess, it being your
first time*: are words you say to defuse him.

TRIPTYCH IN 5 PARTS: ONE PANEL EXPLODED

1.

put up the baby powder: you'll need it later:
& take down the douche: the one shaped like
a grenade: the one that sarge promised would
ship in discreet packaging: but didn't: so now
everyone knows how you spend your time off.
unscrew & fill with water: no soap. start just
south of boiling. wait until the water comes
down to gospel-warm: & squeeze: gently first:
release. repeat until fully cleansed: make sure
you don't forget to thank God for the miracle
of sin.

2.

like any good boy: you've spent your life PrEP-
ping for men you'll never meet: adonis of the grid
with his sheet-rock abs: torso #5: boybreaker 9
in. with just-oiled chest: the guy in grey sweats
with the massive bulge: that one guy who really
likes gunge. like every good boy: you began w/
what was already on hand: summer squash: an
under-ripe banana: the brushes your mom could
never seem to find.

3.

it will be years before you wander into your first
adult store & discover silicone cast into the shape
of man: before you make the switch: baby-oil for
astroglide in the bathrooms of soho: london: b/c
to get properly fucked you'll need some distance
between you & everyone on earth you know: &
even then: only if it's dark: & only if he covers
your face.

5.

for the most part: you remember it all: his eyes:
dark & exacting: jaw: angled & demanding: his
cheekbones that could cut glass: nose: two ears:
thighs for days: lips that would break you by night's
end. what questions does one ask when pinioned
against the wall: arms & legs trussed: like chick-
en in a roasting pan: his body wilting into yours
with the force of one whose god abandoned him
long ago? the truth: you too know a thing or two
about pain: how to fold it over itself: strand-by-
strand like the cat-o'-9-tails he's favored tonight:
until he starts looking like your father shouting
at your mother: *why don't we just take the table-*
cloth & sew it around him? at least then we'll
save some money.

TRIPTYCH IN 5 PARTS ON A BRIDGE AT MIDNIGHT

1.

For the umpteenth time: he checks his phone: waiting for a message
you haven't sent. From here the river bulges: umbilical: bloated x fish
guts & beer cans & cigarettes. There's so many things he wants to tell
you: like how: last week: another man took him home: this one rich:
& old enough to be you. Or how: more often than not: the neighbors
can hear every sound they make: teasing from air the muffled sounds
of bones & breath from sinew & flesh.

2.

He knows he's not the son you signed up for when you married his mother.
He's all feelings: no grit. He cries when others' voices get too loud: prefers
dressing in drag to dressing down deer. He's never liked hunting: but likes
men who carry. Last week: he told a friend he didn't know how to speak to
God anymore: because how could anyone give thanks for a lifetime of pain?

3.

But these aren't the sorts of things boys tell their fathers. Boys tell their
fathers how they bagged a nice one over beer. Boys tell: in great detail:
each thing they did.

4.

In special relatively: Einstein claims that nothing can travel faster than light in a vacuum: that space & time are linked: but he didn't account for the gravity of two bottoms vying for the attention of the same top: or the general relativity of gossip when someone starts a rumor in a gay bar: nor how quickly a twink in heat explodes when he realizes at last call he's going home alone.

5.

He confesses he's here because there's nowhere else he can write his ending without someone asking more questions than necessary: This corner store is the kind of place where people come to be forgotten. Bum or businessman: light hits the same: formican: & soaked in the high-wire hum of indifference. Behind him a man speaks a language he doesn't know: but finds interesting: like how he's always found the sounds words make more sincere than what they mean. Up front the cashier taps his foot in time to the beat of his own impatience while he counts the coins scrounged from his couch earlier tonight. What sort of person pays for their own death in change? What sort of person samples mortality like flavors of ice cream? His problem is he thrives on chaos: so he finds ways to manufacture it: his problem is he's bored with life: his problem is he's one minor problem away from oblivion: his problem: his body is not his own and never will be.

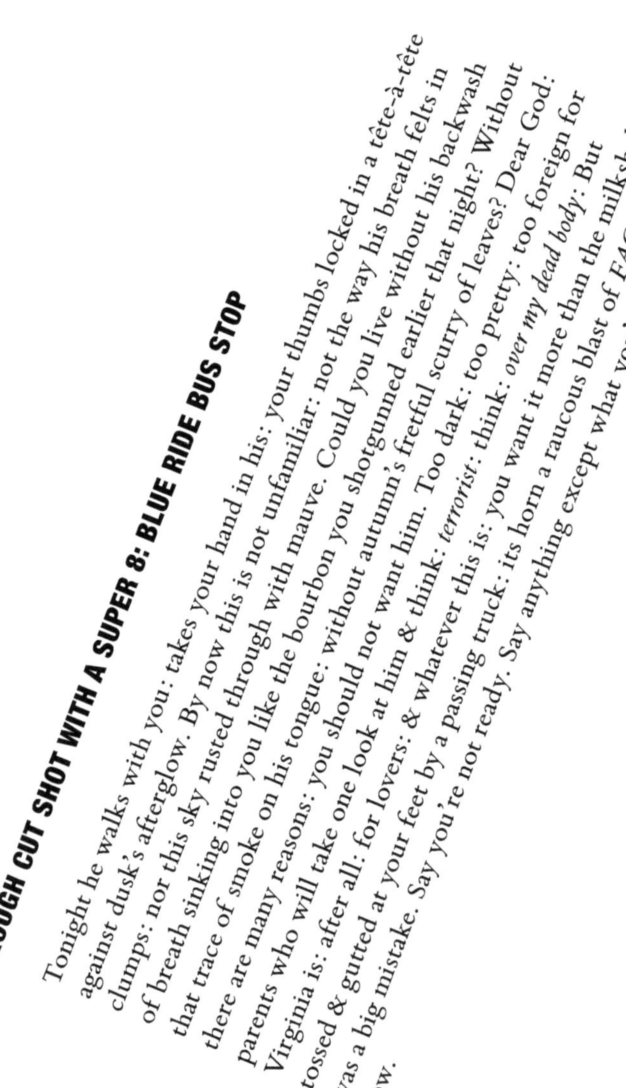

ROUGH CUT SHOT WITH A SUPER 8: BLUE RIDE BUS STOP

Tonight he walks with you: takes your hand in his: your thumbs locked in a tête-à-tête against dusk's afterglow. By now this is not unfamiliar: not the way his breath felts in clumps: nor this sky rusted through with mauve. Could you live without his backwash of breath sinking into you like the bourbon you shotgunned earlier that night? Without that trace of smoke on his tongue: without autumn's fretful scurry of leaves? Dear God: there are many reasons: you should not want him. Too dark: too pretty: too foreign for parents who will take one look at him & think: *terrorist*: think: *over my dead body*: But Virginia is: after all: for lovers: & whatever this is: you want it more than the milkshake tossed & gutted at your feet by a passing truck: its horn a raucous blast of *FAGS!* Say it was a big mistake. Say you're not ready. Say anything except what you're thinking right now.

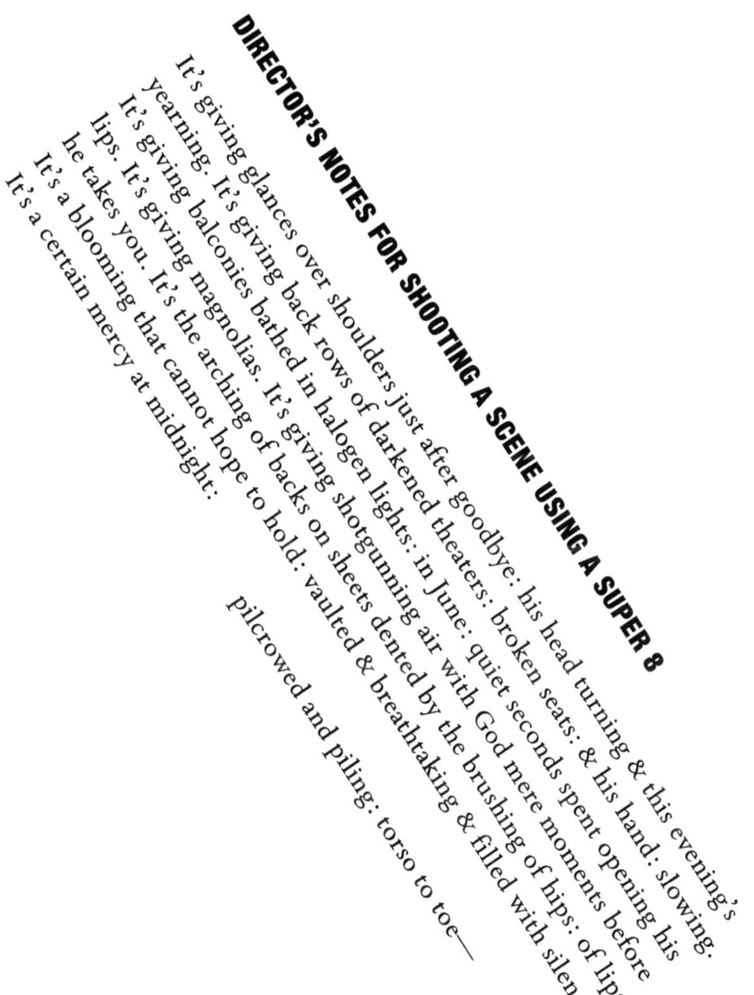

DIRECTOR'S NOTES FOR SHOOTING A SCENE USING A SUPER 8

It's giving glances over shoulders just after goodbye: his head turning & this evening's
yearning. It's giving back rows of darkened theaters: broken seats: & his hand: slowing.
It's giving balconies bathed in halogen lights: in June: quiet seconds spent opening his
lips. It's giving magnolias. It's giving shotgunning air with God mere moments before
he takes you. It's the arching of backs on sheets dented by the brushing of hips: of lips.
It's a blooming that cannot hope to hold: vaulted & breathtaking & filled with silence.
It's a certain mercy at midnight:
pilcrowed and piling: torso to toe—

SOSSITY CHIRICUZIO

I AM THE MOUNTAINS AND THE TUNNEL

SOSSITY CHIRICUZIO (SHE/THEY) IS A FAT FEMME OUTLAW POET, A WORKING CLASS CRIP STORYTELLER. WHAT HER FRIENDS' PARENTS OFTEN REFERRED TO AS A BAD INFLUENCE, AND POSSIBLY STILL DO. A LAMBDA FELLOW AND SENSITIVITY READER AT WRITING DIVERSELY, THEY WRITE AS ACTIVISM, CONNECTION, AND SURVIVAL. AUTHOR OF THE MEMOIR *HONEY & VINEGAR: RECIPE FOR AN OUTLAW* **AND THE POETRY COLLECTION** *BOUQUET OF THORNY ROSE*, **THEIR WORK CAN ALSO BE FOUND IN A VARIETY OF PUBLICATIONS INCLUDING** *SALTY*, *ROOTED IN RIGHTS*, *THE RUMPUS*, *LIBRARY JOURNAL*, *STIRRING*, **AND** *ROGUE AGENT*, **AS WELL AS ANTHOLOGIES LIKE** *THE REMEDY: QUEER AND TRANS VOICES ON HEALTH AND HEALTH CARE* **AND** *NOT MY PRESIDENT.*

HERCULES IS KNOWN TO LIE

I want to read the saga of Echidna
She of lithe scales and ravenous hunger
Mother of monsters, untamed
a beautiful face
telling the story they want to hear
in truth, she danced with selkies slick
with salt water, bellies
rubbing to stardust
whispering secrets stretched long
and sibilant
ship graveyards
and standing stones
gone rust red
the hunger isn't just meat
but a vengeance
close enough to justice
to flavor the bite
they slip their skins
to feast on a naked
that could get them killed
with anyone less trustworthy

FOR THE REMEMBERING

I need to find a spot away from foot traffic, unlikely to be developed, or flood, or fall off the side of a cliff. Someplace someone could find when they need to, but not before then. Someplace I will remember, but not likely return to.

I need someone with a body that can dig down at least 3 feet, maybe more. I need a sturdy chest that will keep bugs and mold and tree roots out. I need plastic, sadly, tightly wrapped.

I need to pick and choose, who to save, who to hope someone else is saving.

How much poetry? How many zines? How many volumes of queer erotica, theory, survival, hope? *Well of Loneliness* but also *Taste This* but also *On Our Backs* but also *Transgender Warriors* but also *Femme Dagger* but also *Care Work: Dreaming Disability Justice* but also so many many how do I choose?

I need them to be found. I need them to be unearthed and unwound and brushed off and cried over and read to tatters. I need to believe we will never need to find them.

AMERICA RULES

Don't drop troublesome truths
out of your broken mouth
you're lucky you can still chew
the pricy scraps
don't compare wages or talk back
to the doctor or the judge
or the cop or the boss or the
list is so long
don't validate ideation
the reasons it resembles escape
nobody is supposed to feel their body
is absolutely theirs
don't share recipes for pregnancies
and administrations
you don't want to carry anymore
only illusions of choice for sale
your body needs to fit
in the profit margins
squeezed tight like coal
or dinosaurs
your bones will be used
to build a yacht
best hope is they fracture
in the rage of a killer whale

NEURAL SYNCHRONY

Thick, thin, thick again, running through my fingers with a soothing regularity. Weaving through the wires I strung, the shape I made. Slippery in the hand, prone to warping, growing stronger the more I push into place. These hours spent with my looms anticipated like romance, reveled in like hedonism, spent and sore and glowing upon completion.

Poetry I can feel, in palates I can't see behind my eyelids. Capturing a scene I remember, an emotion that shattered me open, a prayer, a protest. The best made for some specific someone, holding their essence or asks in my mind, flowing through my fingers into the weft. Held soft and firm there. Ephemeral tremoring beyond the moment.

The pleasure of grounding, of rhythm and repetition. Building texture upon color upon shape, compressing it into meaning. Leaving it wide open, ragged ends, lengths of chain, mesh ripped and gathered and twisted. My hands curled into curls of wire, twisting, pulling, into a shape that stops my breath for a moment. Resting there with wild heartbeat.

Pain finds a quiet corner. Panic lays down. Hours flow past in communion. I am not thinking about all the reasons for a locked door. Not being torn between knowing enough and saturation in despair. Not running lists of all the reasons friends have stopped reaching out, all the mysteries in my medical chart, all the places I may never travel again.

Cradled into the jumble of yarn spread across my altar workspace are oddities, found treasures, and mementos. All of us waiting for transformation. For dismantling and building back up, layer by layer. Frayed and piling soft and firm into the tension, draping and flinging beyond the edges. Creating shapes that fit what is, and what yearns to be.

CRICK CRACK CRUMBLE

does it matter
if I plant the flowers, paint
the kitchen pink
how many tomorrows
to enjoy it, to ever
share it, so many
friends too in love
with normal

Pacing this curated
bubble, as best as limp
allows, as best as pelvic
floor that holds me
hostage, can hold me
up, sore
too much stillness
or motion, a gamble
crick crack
crumble and swollen
everything

eugenic tendrils woven deep
into unraveling radical
community that isn't, always
access that starts and ends
at a ramp to the back door
flashing lights and virus
falling on naked faces
in migraine scented fog
while the crips save
each other, slowly

my rage says burn
it down, but my heart
is a survivor, knows

we need exit plans
this system fails
almost everyone
but also keeps
some of us alive

THE WORLD EATS FEMMES AND I AM LEFT HUNGRY

My heart is a ragged thing. Scars raised raw, fading echoes. There is no song that can convey the sound of her voice. The strength of her choice. She said it's time. She said I love you. She ate the deadly pudding. My ears are empty, the sound is lost.

I swallow, I swallow, I stumble through the day. I make myself eat. I chase sleep into the small hours. I wash my salt burned face. Rearrange it into grace. Swallow my sobs. Change the radio station. Change the subject. The sound is lost. My heart is a ragged thing.

Her voice is part of a chorus. Falling too soon through the cracks of a broken system. Sucked dry and left empty. Poisoned and silenced. A diagnosis of lies. Dismissed when she cries. My heart is a ragged thing, the sound is lost, she is gone. I swallow, I swallow.

I stumble through the day. Looking skyward, seeking hope. I hold the ones still earthbound. I hold myself. I trace the scars. I set them among the stars. I stitch my heart together, tune it to echoes. I sing a ragged song. Her voice is part of a chorus.

PREVIOUS PUBLICATION CREDIT

BOUQUET OF THORNY ROSE (ECHOBIRD, 2025)

THE FLAVORS AND THE FALLING

I have chewed every surface of my tongue to safeguard my skin. Have tasted shame and blood and the spit I did not send flying. Felt it swell like burrs. Tried to swallow it.

I have lain it like a blessing on old wounds and new desires, spring rain bright. Held secrets safe beneath it. Let some unfold and alight the wind. Filled your mouth. Licked your sharp tooth.

The meat of my tongue is pickled in ocean brine and survival. Is sliced at the root and sewn back angry. Is often unsure what is too much truth. Is exhausted from silence and screaming.

The meat of my tongue is a hedonist. A poet. A tamer of manger dogs and horse thieves. Is a builder of bowers and wire tipped walls. Is ready to bathe you and sing your name.

It feeds you chocolate and cardamom. Potatoes anointed in rosemary and butter. The chips that can only be found at that one store. The dumplings that are not quite like your mother's.

It feeds you deep truths that you maybe weren't ready for yet. That you asked for nonetheless. The comfort of lullabies and reflections. The shapes of my trauma and joy. My naked heart.

COMMUNION

I want to feel your tongue between the folds
of my back, delving for mysteries beyond language
hands gripping tight to hips dancing against your chest
while teeth that long for your bicep make do with a pillow
oxygen a joyful sacrifice until you softly roll me over

eyes caressing the waterfall of my belly rising
up to your hungry hands, burrowing
for the wet heat heart of me, tender and fierce
as the formless sounds that sing from my mouth
swollen and curved and shameless

one two three quick slaps to starry constellations
on thighs that have rubbed a thousand miles
through a world that sees me less as my flesh
grows more, that would rob that beauty you see
and leave me hollowed out and stuffed with shame

but your hungry hands write stories of glory
on the scrolls of fat, passed down through
generations of peasants and priestesses
magic spells woven of raw silk and sweet butter
melting on the altar of your tongue

PREVIOUS PUBLICATION CREDIT
BOUQUET OF THORNY ROSE (ECHOBIRD, 2025)

BALANCE

There's a price on these parts
no matter how empty my pockets
the sums of bills upon bills, written
on the outer edge of my eyelid
so it twitch twitch twitches
towards the end of the month
and I squint through the quivers
at this glowing screen, headaches
a couple times a week at least, still
better than a hand gone numb
around my pen, and a poem stillborn
on the paper, nothing but flat blue lines
because the grinding of joints is loud
and frozen all at once, like polar ice
and the keyboard is just a dull ache, cheap
in comparison, though the right forearm
is all used up, left hand on the mouse
coerced into ambidextrous, tiny clicks
that cost hours on the massage table, deep
pressing fingers and elbows to dig out the
ridges of fascia, fused by repeatedly pushing
too far, to find art, and rent, and this voice
that is weighed against bone and vision
and wins every time, this voice
that is all the truest parts of me,
down to the sore depths
until my blood stands still

PREVIOUS PUBLICATION CREDIT
BOUQUET OF THORNY ROSE (ECHOBIRD, 2025)

RECIPROCATING MOTION

Your love
spread cheekbone
to thighbone
rumbling in my ears
like an engine
coming down the tracks
past midnight
stars high above and sparks
flying

bright and high off a curve
rounded almost too fast but not
sliding down these rails like
a hot knife through butter
your back under my nails
chest bellowing like steam
from your belly
rising up my ribcage
pooling

between rise and fall
your forearm piston
rod, cross head axel
sinking deep, superheated
firebox, hard steel
just this side of softening
I am the mountains and the
tunnel, the bridge so high and
swaying

you push through push
and up and through and over
uncharted path where roads
drop off into yards, where trees
stand guard over ancient

tiny glades, untrampled
and your eyes are those flowers
sunlit nectar stories
promising

a bounty of salted pleasure
licked from chin and eyelid
fluttering while the whistle blows
long and loud, my voice
going hoarse and wordless, anyhow
you're listening with your skin
now and palms, my heartbeat
lights the way
radiating

ACIE CLARK

WHAT WE CALL EACH OTHER

ACIE CLARK IS A TRANS WRITER FROM FLORIDA AND GEORGIA, AND NOW HE'S A TRANS WRITER IN ARKANSAS. ONCE, AS A CHILD, HE SAID "I'M A BOY," BUT THE WEEK PRIOR HE HAD SAID "I'M A HORSE," SO THIS CAUSED SOME CONFUSION. HE FIGURED IT OUT. HIS FIRST COLLECTION, *SMALL TALK*, **WAS SELECTED BY DERRICK AUSTIN (WHO APPEARED WAY BACK IN** *ASSARACUS ISSUE 12*) **FOR THE NEW SOUTHERN VOICES POETRY PRIZE AND WILL BE PUBLISHED BY HUB CITY PRESS IN FALL 2026.**

PSALM FOR FORT LAUDERDALE

1 In the beginning, a softer beast felt possible.
I licked my teeth deciduous. Down sprouted
Over the field of me.
2 When the altar-boys said *come*, I crawled, & we
Wove wreaths of sea-grass, foxtail barley, the hair
We sheared from our own heads.
3 We ate our way into liturgy. If the body
Does become what it makes of itself:
4 I was tangerines, key limes, what spilled
From the cups of their waists.
5 Thorough in my misunderstanding, I called this
A choir, a brotherhood—the blue bandana tied
Over my eyes: a curtain between us.
6 Every desire was a confession to be completed,
Wiped clean by each other's open palms.
7 I thought, *we play so rough to love so gently.*
My head held underwater. A roman candle
Aimed at whoever's chest.
8 & what is a little blood to wet the punch,
Or a fistful of hair to notice how long yours
Has gotten?
9 Besides, I learned long ago, in a different church,
The same lesson: *It's not a Eucharist until the holy thing*
Has been consumed.
10 I know this is not just any meal. I take to my knees.
I welcome my teeth. I offer up my tongue.

PREVIOUS PUBLICATION CREDIT
WUSSY MAGAZINE

FAITH HILL

There's a hill where there hadn't always been a hill,
in this part of the country that I try to believe.
In the trying I've hidden a hope. The hope I have
hid all these parts of me. This part of this country
lets me hide here, out of hate or love, I can't be sure.
Hiding is like being held, but a little tighter. I hide
in rivers, in fields, in woods, green and gray, made known
or strange by the light. I use the words I have to talk
about the woods with the woods. Without words,
the woods let me loose from language.
The woods and I don't talk about this country.
The woods and I make silence together.
God's mouth spills out sound in rain all over,
indivisible in the sense that we are always apart.

Indivisible in the sense that we are always a part
of the union we made out of our separate selves,
not long ago, at the edge of this country that does
not believe in us. We come to each other,
God spilling out of the sounds we found
in each other: we fuck and God watches,
without judgment, as if we were any other animal.
In my body my loving is a blessing and I thank God for it,
for you, for your single earring chiming, changing
the world with the words it speaks into the ear
of my palm. To write a word is to create a world
in which that word can mean what one needs it to.
We both chose the words we call to each other with:
these names I have to believe God knows.

These names I have to believe God knows,
though the state calls to us with words we never say.
I hid in a name in a state in a body in this country.
These hiding places are a privilege: my baby body got
called a citizen, a woman, given a name to be called.

This country invented a white god to govern it. They tell
that guy everything. For three decades I've been trying
to tell this story another way; asked to prove to this state
with language, to petition, to pray their prayer:
I hereby swear or affirm I am filing with this Verification,
and the facts stated in it are true. I do not intend
to use this name change to deprive anyone of any
right. Signing with my dead name, *the Petitioner asks that*
the Petitioner's name be changed as provided above.

The Petitioner's name changed as provided above,
on earth as it is in heaven, in God's image, to have
and to hold, forever and ever, we give thanks to thee, amen.
I believe in a God who loves everything even though
each day I catch myself believing everything a little less.
An elder once told me being trans is like the air
in between God and ghost, but I would be content
to be the breath passing over your tongue
as you say, again, you've got to go now, I know,
goodnight, it's so late where you are. Where I am
the rain sounds like a word said over and over
by a God with my accent in this part of the country
I am if nothing else together with
on this hill where there hadn't been a hill,

I do,
I still have some faith.

IL SOLITO PAROLE

I believe I loved you
from the moment I sent you the Sandro Penna poem
where he kisses his lover's armpits, and you went right
to the library to borrow his collected,
but I didn't know how to know so I called the knowing *belief.*

Once, the world was formless and empty.
What was form then? Did earth become
a form in forming, or did it form from form itself?
This is impossible to know. *That's part of it*, you'd say to me.

In the first conversation we had alone, you asked how
I lived with the habitual contradictions,
what I could explain, but hadn't chosen to change.
We were both still drinking. It was cold in Philadelphia,
still so early in what became a long year.

I wish I could say one doesn't manage, or that it's unbearable:
an examined life bearing its awareness, but it wasn't.
I mean, I did manage. It was my life
and I lived it, thinking I knew what I had only come to believe.

In one translation of the poem, summer fails,
and in another it just goes wrong.
At your wedding, I didn't say *don't do it*,
and I'll regret that silence long
after you've left them and it's June again,

so we spend our days on poems,
on the phone, trading pages, not drinking,
and summer joins the usual words
we say to know what we mean.

TEMPERANCE

When I was young   I lived   in the river house

I didn't know   how to die   yet

but I liked   the privacy   of the earth   so well

Us boys   dug holes   sat in them   we picked red berries

for the sweet   harm   how they popped   yellow

How one boy   (shorter than me)   once   spilled

himself   in my hair   to prove   I was less   than him

his small penis   hanging above   a rhododendron branch

I was a boy   the way   a snake   is

a mother   with   another creature's egg   in its mouth

When I say   *the boys I grew up with*   I mean

I spent   each long summer   swallowing   the same egg

PREVIOUS PUBLICATION CREDIT
PUERTO DEL SOL

SUBMISSION

My body can be myself and I can be a place to be,
somewhere another body can go.

When I typed out the yes I had to say,
I did so from a field. I went to his place

and he placed himself inside the place I am.
I wanted to be inside of being inside,

and to exceed myself through being entered.
Did he say that he was mine to use,

or did he say that he would use my using?
The conversation takes place like the image of a singer

as a mirror is sung to, or an imitation
of someone else singing, or someone singing

behind someone standing silent,
moving their mouth for another's song.

Use loosens the lock of *I* that is kept latched:
I open this door to call myself forth, to cull

from my calling my inside self who dreams elsewhere.
Alone in that field, standing at the edge,

standing at the edge of the field of what can be
spoken, there is always this self speaking,

watching what I want be gathered, bailed by
that cord-coarse hold of self over self, reaping

what I can not bear to ask for; I can not bear not to ask.

SIDETRAXX

At the only gay club in Traverse City, my hand finds his
forehead and fingers find my tongue before I think to not taste

his sweat, here where he can see me, watch me wanting
what has not been named enough to ask him for.

Sobriety demands a definitive: you can't unhave anything
from having happened: what is wanted cannot be

cleaved from the task of asking for it. There was once
a line in me: what I could imagine choosing

and what I might be capable of doing or having done to me
while residing in that other self made possible by drinking.

Capable, as if I could ever escape the consequences of the self-denial
slicing paths in me like fishing line cast up into so many branches

while I stood, still there by the creekside, wanting what I had
not given myself permission to want. What I wanted

(to get rid of this line) demanded I lose what I'd been losing,
to lose the loss of not being able to lose myself.

Naked to my reality, nothing made me touch him or let touching
come easy. That night, that taste: I still remember the taste.

ADDRESS

You say exactly what you mean in all your poems
but I still have no idea what it is you're trying not to tell me. I lie

in the grass, reading your horny poems about other men on my phone.
In this one, there's something you want someone else to want.

The you you're addressing hasn't touched the poetic-I you are.
It's obvious where this is going, though it hasn't become apparent

if we're going to sleep together first. I think you've considered it,
but I'm not like the men in your poems, those city

cis boys with theater degrees. I'd be satisfied to be your reader
who always hears about what happens in these rooms

full of men singing to each other, your voice coming through the glass
of each closed moment I see through your poem's curved glass,

the shape of air when air is heat, a list of reasons when I have a while.
Hey, you. I have a while. I have all summer to get it wrong,

to figure out what I want just in time to get to not have it,
but "it" isn't about that, are you? No, there are words

for what I want from you. I want you to tell me
already. I want you to let me finish.

GETTING OUT OF BED ON A JANUARY NIGHT

After Ellen Bass

Standing to go. I can't help it. Moving my arms.
Eyes to there. Where he is yes here he is. Yes
he is again. The down of his body beside.
The space left by my body. Tonight's cold breathes
hard. Against the window but inside. That heat
of his air is a solace that stands still. He wrote
a book a while ago. In the book someone says.
Air is more like water than it is like nothing.
I didn't know him then. But I love who he was.
Silent in his room. Saying that to no one yet.
He's writing a new book. It's set on the moon.
I get to visit him there. To see. The story take place.
The story I'm telling. Takes place. Takes a lot of places.
This room. This night. All waiting to be explained.

MY FAVORITE ART-HISTORICAL CONSPIRACY ABOUT FRANCESCO DEL COSSA, THE GENERALLY UNREMEMBERED 15TH CENTURY ITALIAN PAINTER, IS THAT HE WAS A TRANS MAN.

My second favorite is that there's a self-portrait hidden in a fresco he did for Duke Borso d'Este, a last touch he added before asking for more money: a little shadow trying to paint himself into the government conscience.

If this is right, it's the only image we have of him. If not, we have nothing. No surprise I can't help but picture Cossa like me, tunic off on the porch after a long day of trying to say it, chest let loose, having a cigarette beneath a spider's web turning the color of smoke and now noticed there above our heads.

How beautiful! Beauty, who gets to decide. In my apartment the keyholes all got painted over, but brass peaks beneath white matte, still hollow, still in there: all those teeth that remember the chew of turning.

Tell me, angel of history, did he sleep in the same room he painted in? Who was waiting for him at the end of those long days spent painting frescoes on the walls of a rich man's second palace, paid poorly for his work and by the square foot?

Who should I picture in his bed? I have to admit I'd love Cossa less if I chose to believe he was straight and cis. I'm still waiting to see if I'll disagree with myself about this.

Is art rendered unsuccessful if its worth or relevance undermines or is determined by context? Last night I watched another lesbian movie written and directed by a straight cis man. It wasn't bad, but was it a lesbian movie, or just about lesbians? I was once a lesbian, I mean it, I knew what I wanted based on who I was and when I became something else I wanted both different things and the same things differently.

If I was once one of his models, half-naked, half-asleep, not wholly but not not a man, like I wonder if he was, could Cossa have loved me?

I ask and ask the angel of history, talking to Cossa as if he'll walk through history's door to my room to answer. If he did, I'd say *Frankie, really, come to bed, come to bed! Leave your little tunic there on the chair beside mine.*

GEMINI

After Francesco del Cossa's Triumph of Apollo

At the park, I'm holding a book and in the book there are two boys holding each other. You're holding a book too, reading an essay, one of Didion's, about underground news. You tell me about it while I look at the boys holding themselves together at the arms, their hands tied by their fingers, half a sun between their chests. The sun seems to have set, to be setting. I tell you I think the boys are heaven: their two bodies make a pair of wings, a maple seed in flight. In the painted air surrounding them, nameless men bless one another with their horns, hands, faces. The sun is sliced by an absence that slices one of the boys, too. The unsliced boy is watching the sliced boy watch me watch you. Sight always happens in fragments, figments of what else there is to see when I turn my face from you back to the boys. The book shows the boys *particolare*, which is to say, concerning a small part. I am concerned about the boys, their small parts fading, eroded by time, by the fumes of the factory that gave way to the fresco underneath the paint. I'm learning that's what happens to most art: a building is sold and a wall is painted, then the building is sold and the walls get painted and the building is sold and yet, here, this once: the paint sloughs off and someone notices a face looking through the centuries of paint, a glimpse of the fresco with the boys of which the boys are but one small part of a small part: a moment in a hall of seven legible months in a 1400s pleasure palace turned tobacco warehouse turned museum. Turning the pages of the book, I can see the boys in context. The boys hurtle over a space that was once a field being farmed and is now the absence of a field. Do the boys then become the field, or are they the sky, or some heaven the sky belies? Oh God, James, I'm concerned about all of our small parts, about what I might forget, about the absences always at the edge of these hands we use to hold together this small heaven between us. Your heart holds the wrist of my heart.

WILLIAM LEO COAKLEY
ANTLERHOOD

WILLIAM LEO COAKLEY IS A QUEER BOSTONIAN POET OF IRISH HERITAGE WHOSE WORK HELPED SHAPE PRE-STONEWALL QUEER LITERATURE. ONE OF HIS EARLY POEMS WAS AMONG THE FIRST GAY EROTIC PIECES TO APPEAR IN A NATIONAL MAGAZINE—PRECEDED ONLY BY AN EARLIER POEM BY AUDEN. HIS WORK HAS SINCE BEEN PUBLISHED WIDELY, FROM *THE PARIS REVIEW* **AND** *THE GAY & LESBIAN REVIEW* **TO** *THE IRISH TIMES* **AND VENUES AS FAR-REACHING AS CHINA. HE FREQUENTLY GIVES PUBLIC READINGS IN NEW YORK AND LONDON. COAKLEY SHARED 48 YEARS WITH HIS LATE PARTNER, THE ACTOR, WRITER, AND ACTIVIST ROBIN PRISING. TOGETHER THEY RAN HELIKON PRESS, WHICH PUBLISHED, AMONG OTHERS, THOM GUNN.**

LAST CALL

As the lights dim and flicker
and the coupled start to leave,
discrimination fades:
yes, that one will do.

In the cab home
you struggle to make sense
of who you both are,
of what the night portends.

In bed you exchange secrets
and sometimes forget his name,
resort to: "Amigo,
let me turn you this way."

All night you change positions:
nothing is left out
that you have practiced,
that you remember.

At table in the sleepless morning,
coffee burns your tongue.
At the door, you say:
"Ring you next week"

and when you step back
to sit on the sofa alone,
you find his number
and press DELETE on your phone.

THE ALTAR OF SODOMY

In the great hall he rushed to the altar,
Dionysus the golden image above it,
determined to reign as the high priest.

Stick out your tongues, boys,
in anticipation not derision, submission;
or lie prone on the marble pew
like sculpted Greek heroes without their stone hearts,
the congregation busy about us,
ready to join the orgies of ecstasy
religions never have offered you.

HE

after the photographs of Raymond Navarro

On the streets he is always there,
his back towards me, sometimes naked as sin,
a tattoo screaming Mother or Eat Me or Death
or spreading wide its wings like the angel inside him,
his hair extreme or curled like a Greek god's;
and when he turns, his torn shirt
reveals one nipple's tightness
no-one has bitten or kissed.
I hold my breath and take him
alive in the dim light
to keep him with me forever.

NIGHT THOUGHTS FROM ABROAD

Almost asleep, I turn the light off,
seeing you again in your Roman colors,
before the castle lovers still leap from,
your student's arm fearfully straight behind you.
How many men have fallen and risen for you—
and, ah yes, women too.

What can I do
but love you from a distance?—
as if it were late summer,
the beach on fire in the sun
and I the year's last guest at the Palace,
sitting on top of the dunes,
watching the young man, naked and stronger than riptides,
leap into the surging Atlantic
one more time.

RIDING SCHOOL

after the drawing by Rico Labbé

In harness for the ride, he lies in wait,
His cock extended, ready for your tongue.
Lick the balls first, rise slowly to the root
And then engorge it, keeping it in trim
For sport more energetic and more pleasurable.
Sit on it, roll in knots of his desires,
Hang from the bar, swing in his leathery sling—
He'll keep you busy long into the night.
If light creeps in, no sleep is guaranteed.
You always said, 'A good fuck's what I need.'

BUTTONS

Buttons, my aunt insisted, the jewels of the poor,
And spread her treasures out—yes, I could play with them.
How I believed her: the abalone's pure
Rainbow refulgence! Now my thoughts stay with them
Like childhood memories: languorously I track
The leathered lifelines sewn into a globe,
My uncle's great-coat's manly anchored black,
The pale-green jade replacement for her robe.

That sailor once, the one before the flood
Of history dried up, made me count them first
As I undid them; I stopped, distracted, at four,
And slid the rough wool off. I've not lost my thirst
For buttons since—I hear my aunt behind me
With button boxes, in which, forever, you'll find me.

LETTER TO ROBIN

At the concert you are beside me as always,
music in your eyes, the echo I hear still.

Your advice taken,
I found a man young enough to love
and I share him with others. As you knew,
love is contagious.

But I am less solid than you,
I build my new world of removable bricks.

Would you laugh at the stories they tell of me now?—
all true to life.

NIGHT LETTER

to the memory of Ari Darom, dancer of pure energy and Dionysian promise, born 12 March 1943, died at the year's turning, 1983

Ah my dark bird, your arms poised in flowering flight,
Is it you sunk to this cage of little bones
Dancing, white, white, white in the pure, cold, waters?

ADAM'S SONG

When I was tired,
they took her out of my side;
I woke to that sweet weakness, loss,
and found a new animal pacing the grass—
we paced together, O
what a world it was.
We fed us on my vanity;
hers pulled us down,
down to this earth of death.
While we live, we live
in the moist places, the after-rain
mushrooms sprout like sins.
I keep her for her pains, she breeds:
I who held the one soul alone
watch its dilution into daughters and sons;
the world grows heavy with my diminishing.

FISTING

When I bend over you,
my fingers becoming a fist inside you,
I am no master to fear.
I will lead you slowly
into the woodlands of longing
like a faun beginning to burst
the first buds of antlerhood
and we will find a quiet spot
the sun has forced itself into
where we will lie down together
to melt the ice of our separateness.

AUGUST HEAT

In Paris once, the night coming on,
I caught you in the hedged maze
with desire's probing fingers
—not the endearments whispered later.

Naked in bed, the sex acrobatic,
your rival the August heat,
I held back sleep till dawn,
letting the light reveal you to me whole.

Wandering the noon mist,
the cobbled streets deserted,
we began to find each other.
By every door I held you in my arms.

SAFER SEX

Every day I stop and stare
at the windows where you were,
every day the blinds are drawn
even though your light has gone

and the shadows that I see,
grieving domesticity,
are the mother and the bride,
bodies that you moved inside,

like my body when we fled
homes to our more dangerous bed.
Now the safer grave will take you—
may some heavenly body wake you.

ORPHEUS AND THE JESTER

for Osmani Garcia

They forget the boys, Orpheus
(Who would not remember first
The conquest of Death,
The vanity that loses everything?).
They forget the boys, Orpheus, the beautiful ones,
the dwarf with beguiling eyes
like a King's Jester who taught you to laugh again.
You vanquished even the great god of Grief
To sing inside them.

ON THE CLIFF

for Edgar and David

I have not come for a refuge—
from my solitude I follow your breathing
to where you lie hidden
on the rocks beside me.

When I stand over you,
you are a man of the world
I hardly know, but a man naked,
in the sun, in the salted air,
ready to play the variations,
the music of desire.

Inside each other
we forget everything
except what is united in ourselves.

Hold the heat within you:
the lavas will merge at the cliff's edge
to flow together into the steaming sea.

SPACES

We choose our own names, Natalio, our own lives,
born again in a new country,
Spain still raging in your blood, your sun-tinged skin.
We are not content with the world we see around us—,
we invent the spaces where life can thrive and go on,
like a plant that grows by the window,
its green aroma quickening the air we breathe in.

If you paint me,
make me a spiral that twirls up to you,
a clown with two heads who looks at you from all angles,
an ass that carries you.

JOHN COMPTON
COCK LIKE A SHOTGUN

JOHN COMPTON (B. 1987)—GAY, COUNTRY, AND HAS DEVOTED LIFE TO POETRY. A REBEL, WON'T BE QUIETED DOWN, AND OPINIONATED. A HOMEBODY, ANIMAL-LOVING, EMDASH ENTHUSIAST! HE IS THE AUTHOR OF 20 BOOKS/ CHAPBOOKS WHO LIVES IN KENTUCKY WITH HIS HUSBAND JOSH AND THEIR DOGS AND CATS AND MICE. HIS LATEST FULL-LENGTH BOOK IS *MY HUSBAND HOLDS MY HAND BECAUSE I MAY DRIFT AWAY & BE LOST FOREVER IN THE VORTEX OF A CROWDED STORE* **PUBLISHED WITH FLOWERSONG PRESS (DECEMBER 2024); HIS NEW FULL-LENGTH BOOK** *HOUSE AS A CEMETERY* **IS OUT FROM REBEL SATORI PRESS (MARCH 2026). YOU CAN FIND HIS BOOKS, SOME POEMS, AND OTHER THINGS HERE:** *HTTPS://LINKTR.EE/POETJOHNCOMPTON*

MY BODY IS CURVATURE

my body is curvature.
the yielding dome
rises as i lie on my back:

the shape of earth.
my lover sleeps
in the valley of my legs.

a small fox of hair
burrows into my thigh—
nesting in his dreams.

the moon, a thin slice
of precooked sausage,
is hazed behind

egg whites
clouding the sky;

the sun breaks
sunny side up
about to wake him.

the shell of his mouth
cracks with a yawn—
an embryo falls off his tongue:

a promise.

he shifts, raises his head.
his face, a hydrangea—
white petals adjust;

bloom—as he maneuvers
cross-legged
to face me.

our fingers weave
into umbilical cords.

I WATCH PEOPLE WATCH PEOPLE WATCH PEOPLE

i watch people watch people watch people
look at me. i sit
at a bench because my body is no longer new.

i sit at the bench, my vision swirls.
i try to gather myself. my husband
continues shopping. my mind is fatigued.

i watch people watch me watch my cane
laying over my legs. its black metal body
with its three-hoofed foot protruding.

the handle is a duck's bill but more quiet.
the people with their eyes like cameras.
my back slouched like a deflating balloon.

i breathe. i breathe while people watch me.
they breathe. their bodies moving in synchronicity.
i watch people like cattle knowing the way.

my husband finishes, finds me, sits beside me.
        we follow the herd.
we check out. we exit into the world—

only then do i become invisible.
only then do they forget.
only then do they deny. we are animals.

MY EARS RING FROM THE THUNDER. ANXIETY

my ears ring from the thunder. anxiety
    grows
like a cumulonimbus cloud.   & expands
disconnecting the ceiling   from the frame—
    the wind knocks the door from its hinges.
    heavy rainfall occupies the room,
destroys the walls.

        i sign
        the divorce papers.

you take the dogs.   give me the cats.
you take the house.   i grab the keys to the car.
you acquire the bills.   i pull from the driveway
                            on two bad tires
and ten thousand miles overdue for an oil change.

my therapist said: you lived two different lives.
the intersection never opened
after it shut down for road work.   the orange cones
kept getting in the way.   made u-turns
normal.   delays made things change.

my cats fight in the backseat.
    they learn from what they're taught.
i hear one yell: i can't wait until the supreme court
dissolves our marriage
    so it will be easier for me to leave.
        the other is left grasping.

I IMAGINE JOHN ASHBERY READING MY BOOK INSTEAD OF DYING

john ashbery laid my book
on his desk, his face
aligned with the cover.

his fingers stitched neatly,
binding his hands.
his eyes extending their reach.

he sat, soundlessly,
listening to david, in the other room,
gather produce for a vegetable soup.

the pantry door creaked gently,
dropping a poem into the air.
he breathed, a subtle groan—

the sound of preparing.

john lingered at the title page,
letting the poems simmer:
a breath caught in his cheek.

he slid his finger across *trainride*,
met the corner of the page,
& turned to "felicity."

he understood the mathematical equation
referencing a blowjob.
his smile creased like a dog-ear.

THE JUKEBOX ANTHEM & THE DISCOVERY OF HETEROSEXUALITY WITH RELIGION

i am gay for the dead i was blamed for

•

i hear about your new faith & how your body became
another vessel for representation

•

i feel starved from the rearrangement of your conscience

•

i taste smoke that brought annihilation to our house

:

sitting in a motel room

•

on the mattress

•

imagining a man. a woman

•

sex

•

dirty sheets. sweat

•

real names, concealed

•

a fake orgasm. mouth

•

parted

•

cock like a shotgun

VIBRATION BETWEEN THE THIGHS

the wind
blows the dust
from
your ears

catches you
off guard

pulls
the howl
from your throat

DON'T WORRY, IT'S VALENTINE'S DAY

it's hard when everything's falling apart,
my darling.

your slumber into melancholy
etches more daunting images

on the infernal surface
of this nullified

mannequin skull

you've assembled to store
your mental health—

but the engraver, pushed too hard,
broke through bone:

your suicidal hunger
discharges.

the house is quiet.
the thunder of a lonely train

rages. its cargo loose.
the rattle like some snake

come to wrap itself
around my neck:

a scaly lace.
it pricks, tightening.

STUDY OF FIGURE X

twink
kneeling over

the edge
of my bed

i sit between
his smooth legs

his ass
in the air

like an altar
—i shove rosary beads

into his hole
and use the crucifix

to pull them free.
he moans

my hymns.
i light candles

on his cheeks
to send

sins
to heaven.

STUDY OF FIGURE XIII

i applied the brakes,
hydroplaned,

skid in reverse
through a culvert,

tipped vertical
and continued into a field.

i tilted my head, and—hugged
by my seatbelt—

i looked down.
the passenger window

became a garden bed
full of confusion.

i touched
my husband's face

in an attempt to persuade
the flowers

he was hiding in his mouth
to bloom.

AFTER REALIZING MY NAME MEANS "GIFT FROM GOD"

i represent something that is familiar to somebody. a garden
too invaded by creeping thistle. i must be sick.
i must be eroded.
my body, muddy and moist, leaving me bloated and drowning.
the water wasting out my pores, the religious patrol
with contempt. resentment falling from their mouths.
it is too harsh
to not be a choice: *you belong in hell.*

may their teeth resume chewing.
may my bones be more charming.
at least the bones can't look gay; the bones
can fashion themselves normal. off-white and not pink.
you can't tell by examining which bones
wore what skin suit and by that i mean
the word *fag* is not engraved in the bones.

gay is a *death sentence. that* body is a *funeral.*
the body represents growth and procreation.
the bones, the bones, the bones tell you no secrets, no truths.
you are more beautiful when silenced.

EZRA FOX

THE FLOWERS PEOPLE LEAVE

EZRA FOX IS A BEST OF THE NET NOMINEE WHO LIVES AND WRITES IN SAN FRANCISCO AND HOLDS AN MFA IN CREATIVE WRITING FROM INDIANA UNIVERSITY. A TIN HOUSE AND LAMBDA LITERARY FELLOW AND A RECIPIENT OF THE LILI ELBE MEMORIAL SCHOLARSHIP FOR PROMISING TRANSGENDER WRITERS, EZRA'S WORK APPEARS IN *TRIQUARTERLY*, *THE PINCH*, *FOURTEEN HILLS*, **AND ELSEWHERE. ADDITIONALLY, THEY WON THE 2025** *WEST TRADE REVIEW* **POETRY PRIZE, AND WAS SELECTED AS A FINALIST FOR POETRY PRIZES FOR** *PALETTE POETRY*, *BELLINGHAM REVIEW*, **AND** *BIRDCOAT QUARTERLY*. **MORE OF THEIR WORK CAN BE FOUND AT** *EZRAFOX.NET* **OR ON INSTAGRAM** *@EZRAXFOX*.

AS BOYS DO (I)

The boys are all warm cheeks, round
from the dinners their mamas make,

as they pass a depleting bottle along
the rusted railroad track, tipsy with

the twinge of getting older, still babies,
they roughhouse at the ravine's ledge.

A sight worth seeing, had it been daylight,
had the trees not been melting tombstones.

When the burning tickle of booze drifts
into a somber ache, or, once their little games

grow boring, the boys allow silence to spread
between them as a distant rattle grows.

The bridge sways and swells violent,
the sudden sobering of a whistle's howl,

the engine hot and heavy, its light a halo gaining.

Perhaps they sucked in their soft bellies,
curling toes, palms pressed in prayer.

Perhaps they jumped.

Three boys suspended mid-air,
caught between flight and falling,
not the certainty of gravity.

Or perhaps, as boys do, when the burn
of booze ignites a hot arrogance

that makes boys feel like men,
they will puff out their chests,

howl at the moon despite its newness,
and each bet their last five dollars

on who can remain on the tracks the longest.

How three boys will dig their heels
to claim victory. How they will feel
that when the time comes, they will have time.

AS BOYS DO (II)

The boys feel the bridge
shake and know suddenly
what their mothers know,
that the train is coming

with its single eye,
and one boy reaches
for the other's hand first,
because he has known him
since kindergarten,
since they both pissed themselves
during the fire drill,
and he squeezes back,
and they are crying now,
or laughing, it's hard to tell
the difference
when you are sixteen
and drunk
and the train is so close

you can feel it in your molars,
and the third says *I love you guys,*
which makes them
laugh-cry harder,
because boys don't say that,
except when they do,
except when the bridge is shaking
so hard their knees buckle,
and they hold each other
the way their mothers held them,

the way they will never
hold their own children,
and the light is so bright
it erases everything

but the warmth
of another palm,
another pulse,
another boy who is afraid.

The bridge shakes.
Their mothers are asleep
in their beds. Someone's crying.
Everyone's crying.
The bottle rolls.
They hold so tight
their ribs might crack.

The train screams.
They are so young.
The train screams.
They hold on.

O ENGINE OF MY OWN UNMAKING

My grandfather is teaching me to gut a fish, his hands slick with the silver of not-speaking, and the boys are holding or not holding. I can't tell if I am the train or the track or the light that makes them visible for one more second, one more. I keep trying to be the light but I am the tunnel. I am all throat and forward. I am what comes to swallow. O my body is a locomotive and also the thing it hits, also the moment before, stretched so thin it becomes a wire I balance on, and my father's father never held my father and so my father's hands are stones he skips across water, they land and land but never sink, and I am trying to drown them, I am trying to hold what they could not, I am one boy's throat and the word dies there, becomes a train whistle, and the boys' mothers are folding and folding, they are origami-ing their sons back into existence, and I am thinking about birth, how it is also a kind of train, how you cannot stop it once it starts, how I might open and pour out boys who will refuse to jump, who will inherit my silence like a house with all the windows nailed shut, and, O I am the house and the hammer and the hand that swings it. I am one boy's palm almost reaching, and then pulling back to punch the other boy's shoulder because touch is only allowed if it leaves a bruise, if it can be called a game, if no one has to admit the train is real. The train has always been real. I have been running from it and toward it my whole life. I derailed myself to survive. I jumped before the bridge. I am still jumping. I am mid-air right now deciding if I killed the boys or freed them, if the coin in my pocket is fare or inheritance, if I owe the boys anything or if they owe me, trying to recognize what looks back, trying to love it, trying to hold its hand the way the boys could not hold each other, the way my grandfather could not, the way the track holds the train, which is to say it doesn't it just allows—the weight to pass over, it just bears the impact and remains, and I am trying to remain. I am counting the flowers people leave and the flowers they don't. I am the bridge still shaking years later. I am a body in a kitchen learning what's inside, learning to remove it, and the boys are suspended mid-air still, they are always mid-air in my mind, and I am trying to reach them but my hands are my father's hands, are stones, are never quite touching, are almost, are almost.

A WAY WITH THOSE HANDS

If you've never heard
if my son was gay I'd kill him,

while getting a line up and said nothing,
you must've never had a single blade razor

resting against your neck, in the hand
of the barber who said it.

You must've never felt the closet come
to swallow you back in. A bomb shelter,

a lowering of the larynx. I felt the heat,
his spit landing on my forehead changing me.

But, I mean, my god, he's got such a way
with those hands. I am his for the hour.

The clippers gliding a steady buzz,
his fingers at my neck. Our faces so close,

I can smell his breath. I make memory
his crooked tooth, his protruding jaw,

and myself in his eyes: caped and at his mercy.
He will whisper a sweet *sorry man*

for his roughness. Lips at my ear,
so only I can hear his mistake,

his tenderness. If I touch him back,
everything about me will be true.

So, I will watch his hands, wait
for the invitation. After blowing me

dry, we will touch one another,
and dap up a wordless thank you.

Bro, that haircut looks so good on you.
I mean it bro, you look really nice.

To which he means: *you're welcome,*
or, *I love you,* but *no homo.*

PREVIOUS PUBLICATION CREDIT
SIERRA NEVADA REVIEW

CATCHING FIRE

I am not asking
if David loved Jonathan.
I am asking if the chalice tastes
like metal because someone's
mouth was here before mine.

A thousand years ago,
David was tasting iron
in Jonathan's spit
after battle and now
I'm on my knees
in a church someone forgot
to lock, as his thumb finds
the split in my lip.

Once, there were two men
in a field and the scripture
called them *lovely in their lives*.
Once, someone made this wine
in a factory and boxed it.

There's a country between
his teeth, and mine
are purple. O, scripture
that never names
what it describes.
You gave us *wonderful*
and *lovely* and expected
us not to want.

David cut the corner
of Saul's robe and kept it,
proof he was close enough
to kill, but did not.

WHEN THE TRANS BOY BALLS

after Yusef Komunyakaa's "Slam, Dunk, & Hook"

there was a time
i could mean a girl
hard, cross her over
tangled ankles.
when all my threes
were deep and dirty.
my laces defied gravity
like little bees wings.
wrist flicked, face smug
with swagger. the sun
swishing through its own
netted horizon, glinting
our sweaty brows. and we
could last almost forever
this way. in springy steps,
in this fever dream of grit
and game, and give me
all of your heart and hustle
and what hurts you don't hurt
no more on this court
of layups and lost time.

everything is different now,
except the muscle memory
this body keeps. and i am
no longer a bee, just a flower
petal, pollen dusted off
the back legs of the big boys
who say my shorts ain't baggy
enough for people not to think
something of the way i'd call out
with my wind chime voice.
who say *beautiful*
but *dangerous*.

they must not know
my moves like hot
mercury. game too big
for everything about me
they are afraid of.
now i can't play anywhere,
but in these desolate courts
that hide nothing
beneath the flicker
of street lights, alone,
counting down my own
shot clock, juking out my own
shadow.

PREVIOUS PUBLICATION CREDIT
POIESIS

WHAT THE DARKNESS RENDERS ON THE QUESTION OF PASSING

Origami of half-truths.
Wet stone of shoulder,
salt-lick of streetlight.

Consider the man who lingers
longer than necessity demands—
dusk seeping through collar,
soft as bruised peach.

The pronoun: a migrating bird
wingbeat,
restless.

His eyes searching for permission:
a hand grenade threaded with lace,
pin pressed between milk teeth.

Body out of reach
to his throat's wilderness.
Above us the moon
ensnared in telephone wires.

Consider the nightfall,
how it renders us incomplete.
The muscle memory of keys
between knuckles.

Our shadows threading
their needles through
the skin's assumed fabric.

How some bodies learn
to read darkness differently.

Consider the truth of my body.
    How some revelations
        can turn a compliment
            into a closed fist.

Then consider, how many
have been harmed for less.

PREVIOUS PUBLICATION CREDIT
WEST TRADE REVIEW (2025 POETRY PRIZE WINNER)

LUTHER "LUE" HUGHES
INTO MY MOUTH

LUTHER "LUE" HUGHES (SHE/HER) IS THE AUTHOR OF *A SHIVER IN THE LEAVES* **(BOA EDITIONS, 2022), LISTED AS A BEST BOOK OF 2022 IN** *THE NEW YORKER*, **AND THE CHAPBOOK,** *TOUCHED* **(SIBLING RIVALRY PRESS, 2018), RECOMMENDED BY THE AMERICAN LIBRARY ASSOCIATION. SHE IS THE FOUNDER OF SHADE LITERARY ARTS, AN ONLINE PLATFORM FOR QUEER WRITERS OF COLOR, COHOSTS** *THE POET SALON* **PODCAST WITH GABRIELLE BATES AND DUJIE TAHAT, AND SERVES AS THE POETRY EDITOR FOR** *CHUM NEWS*. **HER HONORS INCLUDE THE RUTH LILLY AND DOROTHY ROSENBERG FELLOWSHIP, THE 92Y DISCOVERY POETRY PRIZE, AND CASCADE PBS'S BLACK ARTS LEGACIES HONOREE. SHE WAS ALSO NAMED MOST INFLUENTIAL BY** *SEATTLE MAGAZINE*. **HER WRITING HAS BEEN PUBLISHED IN** *THE PARIS REVIEW*, *ORION*, *AMERICAN POETRY REVIEW*, *SEATTLE MET*, **AND OTHERS. SHE'S BEEN FEATURED IN** *THE SEATTLE TIMES*, *FORBESWOMEN*, *ESSENCE*, **KUOW PUBLIC RADIO, AND MORE. LUE LIVES IN SEATTLE, WHERE SHE WAS BORN AND RAISED.**

THE MIST IS FRAGILE, BREAK IT

The cherry blossoms I've lauded for years,
their hairy faces slumping against the wind,
fibbed about their beauty. The reason fails
when an orange cat scurries into the yard
of the abandoned house where a shower
of them drama. There are reasons for emptiness.
There is the day the Lord has made for everyone's
death, my mother used to say before hers
was made in the blank San Antonio night
as our family watched her sip from Death's mug.
There is the emptiness of my presence
in her memory, emptiness in the broken suitcase
I towed back after leaving her there to live
out her last and stale days, emptiness
of how I reached the small café on my walk
down 12th Ave, blossom after blossom
taxing my attention. In the café: a painting
of a falsehood forced in blue light, a couple
of teens playing the dozens corner side,
a small child sincerely dressed in black.
Then there is the fullness of the apple I bite into
as a man hoists his voice on the phone,
demanding to speak to his mother's doctor.
Are you stupid, are you fucking stupid,
he asks, his voice stabbing the room red,
the apple redder, my anger reddening with him.
I keep lying about my grief. The trees prove nothing—
their silly deaths and resurrections are tired.
Why didn't I hound when the doctor named it?
Who told me I couldn't dive crown first
into the red sea? The symphony brushes its teeth.
I take my chai tea into my mouth, swish
the man's voice between my cheeks, swallow.

WHEREAS/HOWEVER/NEVERTHELESS

The vanity mirror vomits seeing my face.

Next to my lover, I scale myself.

I open for the wrong man as the married one begs to enter the room.

I: the medication is working. Body: I need more.

In the dream, my mother still breathes like a Southern Woman.

The herd of condolences swallows every drop of water.

He cries into the phone and doesn't know why.

I prefer men jostled inside my mouth—*More, sir. Yes, sir.*

The Book of Loss rivals its movie adaptation; I remove myself from both.

It rains on the fictional side of town, and I'm stuck in the figurative.

My doctor: one tablet by mouth three times a day.

I imagine heaven has three of me: boy, not boy, not-not boy.

In the dream, vultures signature the street in front of Walmart.

My friends are writing books about The Image and The Political.

A woman buys my mother a kale and strawberry smoothie—*This is good, son.*

I place my non-gender inside the locker room when I enter the bathhouse: *Fuck me.*

My family aches for invites to the wedding; I shovel rice into my mouth.

The recipe tells me to chop the ginger root into smaller pieces for morning shots.

A murder of [black leaves] choir the park.

Cherry blossoms wither at autumn's behest.

Her last voicemail says she wants to come home.

My friends buck at the nearest unopened bottle of Hornitos.

Eros shook my mind like a mountain wind falling on oak trees.

His come-churning face in dead silence empties the ache.

Three rotted types of cheese make love in the trash.

I imagine a child pulling the legs off an already croaked spider.

The maximalist hole adorns the vase's head; I rebuke the theory.

Twenty fed up raspberries howl from the fridge.

Grey's Anatomy season 3, episode 17; season 9, episode 10; season 17, episode 5.

A video of blackbirds leaping to the ground desires attention.

Eros is an issue of boundaries.

The yellow rose ages between the room's locked jaw; I fret.

A dead mother thinks her son is still that.

Unsent family photos loiter in email drafts, daily dawdles until the deadline.

~~Motherless~~ Humanless dog tours the park at night.

A plea: *Next time we fuck, I want you to record me.*

Interrupted subscription service—"Change payment method?"

Broken lipstick slurs the drawer red.

*The two lines that start with "Eros" are from *If Not, Winter: Fragments of Sappho* by Anne Carson

FROM THE OPPOSITE END OF THE ALLEY

Outside the bar, the white man I kissed shares a cigarette with my fiancé. The act refuses to escape the mind's curtain call. I deserve what the night has dogeared. Pink lip on the rim, pink paint on the nails. The white they/them sings about a down and out Black mother. I finger my likes for a chuckle or three. The bar that hates us down the street is mentioned beneath the breath of beer. My fiancé orders two shots of tequila. The day wants to linger on my lips. I understand. Sometimes it's hard to keep things alive. *Are we gonna sip this shot?* I nod. The music curtsies before us.

AXIS OF REVERIE

As days dilly-dally, I find myself becoming my mother.
The vanity mirror squirreled in the open den holds little romance.

The arias of silk scarves feverish for frolic in the sun.
Taking a man's last name as my own.

Bring Arrowhead water, I had commissioned my man gift my mother
when they were to meet for the first time. He scintillated

showing me the case of Dasani water. *That's not Arrowhead*, I clucked.
That's not Arrowhead, my mother squawked when he presented it to her.

Churched with glee at our twinning, I ushered him to the bedroom
where we watched *Sorry to Bother You*

and ate yams, collard greens, the perfect turkey,
    a pun of shrimp for kicks.
My mother and her girlfriends gassed The Good Works of God
    in the front room.

As I apply concealer under my eyes and along the quoins of my mouth
almost a decade later, I'm reminded my mother often locked her door

to do her makeup. Maybe for privacy or the beck for aloneness.
I'm hazy how her feathers would taint if she knew I wore makeup now.

The possibility of her anger stroked out with her.
The fact is the workday ahead is unseasoned.

The sun is approaching its shy era.
There's a cackling whisper justifying the fridge.

Motions from the bedroom indicates my husband has awoken.
I lean closer to the mirror to set my mother's face with powder.
    Lock everything in with spray.

THIS ISN'T THE RAINBOW RAVED ABOUT

I sit beneath the defective sky and read the obituary.
The property behind the fence is more thought
than house. I'm virginal when it comes to redlining.
Natural selection. Five-layered cakes. The wind's sassiness
stills my dog stiff. Sometimes being motherless scares me,
the bones of the fact shimmying into the day's falsified peace.
I'm supposed to listen to the congregation of nature,
the corona of patterns purpling into opulence
while my dog studies a crow studying it. Science defines
most black birds a nuisance, but I've been gagged enough.
Suppose nothing else came of today. The day hung
by leisure, suppose there was and there wasn't a need for
Wellbutrin. Jubilee. Requiem. Cloven. Kyrie.
I know things must happen. People masturbate.
Someone eats freshly cooked lentil soup.
There is the perfect gospel song in rotation.
The lake too far to mention.

SEAN PATRICK MULROY

YOUR BROTHER'S FILTH

SEAN PATRICK MULROY IS A WRITER, MULTI-DISCIPLINARY ARTIST, AND FAGGOTRY HAUNTOLOGIST FROM THE AMERICAN SOUTH, WHO HAS LIVED ALL OVER THE WORLD, AND PRESENTLY IN NYC. AN INTERNATIONALLY RECOGNIZED POET, PERFORMER, AND AWARD-WINNING PROFESSOR OF WRITING, SEAN IS A 2013 LAMBDA LITERARY FELLOW, 2018 WRITER-IN-RESIDENCE AT THE KEROUAC PROJECT IN ORLANDO, FLORIDA, AND WINNER OF THE 2020 BUTTON POETRY CHAPBOOK CONTEST. IN 2023, BUTTON POETRY PUBLISHED HIS DEBUT COLLECTION, *HATED FOR THE GODS*.

ANGORAE NOCTIS

The one about your mouth—
a fruit which bleeds when twisted
from the tree.

To taste it is to sleep
within my sleep, which is to say
it's death.

Thinking Of You!

both
the text inside a greeting card
and what will someday kill me.

Your face—a pale stage.

Every other thing, the curtains
closing.

TRITON

The world is too much with us, late and soon...
we have given our hearts away, a sordid boon! —Wordsworth

25 years later, I still think about you and the night we spent together, belly down and side-by-side, stretched out across your carpet, white and new and strangely clean for any teenage boy's room. Birthday party over and your mom and brother both asleep, we lay there with the Abercrombie Quarterly. Bruce Weber's chosen medium: the human body. Floating in between us, undine swimmers, surf boards staged strategically to hide and to reveal their lithe perfection, lifeguards captured lovingly with such ache their green neon velcro flip-flops seemed almost romantic. We held one side of the book each, our eyes widening at every page turned. In the center spread, a long bench which extended all the way across a wooden dock. A pair of lovers, sitting close together, kissing on the left, while on the right a solitary man sat, arm extended toward them, his hand vanishing within the dark-creased binding of the book. On the next page with his back to us—the same man, still alone, but cast in treelike silhouette, unclothed before the ocean, knee-length swimsuit, red Hawaiian floral, wilted wet and held above his head like fruit unreachable and deathly sweet, lust-glistened, muscled curves and ass magnificent, confounding us to silence. I could not imagine what it might be like to look like that, like warmth made flesh, a body without gatherings of fat or softness anywhere, like yours was then, an athlete, junior varsity, your dark hair curling loosely as unfurling smoke from cherub mouth. It was so quiet, suddenly. We went to turn the page in unison; our fingers touched, and then our glances wed like drops of water gliding down the model's back. A snapshot, teenage hormones vaselined across the lens: two friends, just friends, and maybe only one forever captured in the flash. I'd never felt like that before; like I was treading water in a single moment, and might drown. I was afraid. I was a man almost, although I didn't know it yet, and neither of us could've guessed what different lives then surged towards us, whispering white surf and salt-wet foam. You could've offered yourself to me openly—I still wouldn't have known what I should do. You looked away first, laughed a little.
I laughed too.

COWBOY WITH A BLACK EYE

to be read in drawl

It doesn't matter what
he looked like but
he looked like this:
a farm kid,
yellow-haired and young
and liquored up with
missing pills still chuckling
in his gut. No shirt.
A lanky sun burnt frame
embroidered gray in tattoos
fading blue.
You dirty boy, you.
You hold on a bit too long
with every touch.
You ask for more.
You ask too much.
You lust for punishment.

Sing songs of theft for him
who steals the world with
stolen kiss by stolen kiss,
if bruise-betrayed
by what you covet.

You don't blame or love
the boys what beat you up.
At least they touch you with
their hands.
A man sweeter than
pipe tobacco, smoke taste
Stetson aftershave
and simple,
pretty.
Simple taken pretty quick if
he should find he likes it
some when dumb drunk,
ruinous and desperate.
dangerous and worth it.
It was worth it.

GIVING MY FIRST BLOWJOB IN A TRAILER PARK

Steven's mother is a dyke—a biker chick who's out tonight
with her new girlfriend—but she's left her jacket for her son
to wear. Its leather grips the angles of his body
like a tight black fist.
Within its grasp, the gray-eyed boy who'd teach me how to love
the taste of Budweiser—he'd kiss me after drinking it.

We're jealous of each other, and so—sex.

I want a father like his father, shadow only used to bring him
into being, left unseen, the rumor of a storm.

I want this boy, carpenter's son, who's left alone
inside this empty trailer with his mother's tool belt
hanging on the door and gasoline fumes in his hair.

I stamp the cigarette I don't know how to smoke yet
in the brown glass of an ashtray, let him lead me
to his bedroom with an arm around my waist.

He wants my parents' money, so he ruts me in the mouth.
He stumbles to his mom's bed, leaves me buzzing
with the taste of it: the power lines across his lawn.
Electrified, I lie there in his bedroom, shaking
with excitement, fear, my clothes torn, lips raw,
neck flourished with bites.
I must be the luckiest faggot in the trailer park tonight,
knocked out like a prom queen, sleeping in the arms of
nothing but the way he made love to my face.
The way his palms caressed my ears, his voice a bright tiara, set
with nothing but the way he said it: *That's right—good boy*

good boy

good night

FRATERNITY

for the men of Delta Lambda Phi

When I can't be distracted and I think of him, my mother's other son, half-mine by half of blood, sun-fading tattoos, a pill-choked voicemail, long his hair and braided, Harley waiting for him in a locked garage while he does time again—

Half him says he, my blooded code, a phantom wed with smoke. I'm looking where I shouldn't when I find his porno magazines wrapped in some dirty coveralls. *Your brother's filth* comes mother's mutter, but she never fails to send him money when he calls. *Half filth* my bloodline utters, *Family cannot be coincidence.* I am 13, when I begin to dream of brothers who do not exist. We wander neighborhoods in subdivisions full of children, places where I never lived, with storm sewers and sprinkler systems, sword play, freeze tag, hockey played in cul-de-sacs, the last picked scab, clandestine piss in back of someone's half garage and peeking thrill of juvenile risk. *Suppressed but unmistakable as sex and only sex* blood says and I am disappointed in my body. I can love without my prick sometimes. Can shut my ears to bloodspeak, let the fireside of men console me without sex, the wolf what lies in wait for me. I take the first watch for them, guard the night, although at times, a brittle glass, they hold me. Strong the circle, we, our thirty voices raised in song, our arms a chain around each other's shoulders, loud. We sing of love, of bloodless bond, although I freeze when named as such. When someone calls me

Brother— record scratch. The needle buried deeply in his thigh. A silence played behind all men. All else, a weight-borne sigh, an opera of loss and letch, a bloodlife ceaseless. Lonely. My beloved brotherhood, more than a lover could, you made of me, a man, and O! How you have saved me!

THE HANGING OF MAHMOUD ASGARI & AYAZ MARHONI, JULY 2005

I once was pain itself, and proud to carry Hell within me;
by your hand, beloved King, I am transformed into a healer. —Rumi

While Western journalists debate the worthiness of mourning us,
our short lives measured by the nature of apocryphal offense—

we stand before a crowd unsighted, blindfolds tightly crowning us,
suspended in the gallows of a photograph held up by activists and

magazines, each hoping for our finishing to mean a thing more than,
A love once it's unraveled, will not breathe.

When culture can excuse a murder faster than the speed of a caress, or
justify it just as softly, governments twist scripture into windswept

shackles, grip the sin and then its punishment; whether it's insolence
or rape, the fact remains that few alive remember now our names

as once were whispered into prayer by verses of a priest: the slave
become malik, the king his conqueror to hoist on roaring sword.

How like the world, forsaking books, to author them with early ends.
Irrelevant, the men who stare into our death in search
of their own noise.

Ayaz, these ropes they fling about our necks can't hold us
with the same conviction as we held each other, in another life.

Now side by side, our bodies cradle what we craved in secrecy, and
fearfully, we fled. Our war-split lips, a tenderness made mercifully

brief. Let others craft and execute such sentences as beauty and
their hate demand. With childlike weight, we sway until we cease.

We swing together gently on the breeze.

FOR OUR BODIES, HOMOSEXUAL AND AGELESS

First: your friends begin to marry and have kids (and if they're artists, start to make their art about said marriages and kids). All conversation drifts in their direction, and you learn how to be genuinely interested, and later, how to babysit. One night, the chosen family's newest member throws a fit, and witnessing it summons up some memory:

Small you, a mother who refused to pick you up or let you have or else would not forgive. You think,
What year was that?
then maybe say,

My god—she'd only just turned 28.
You see it, finally:

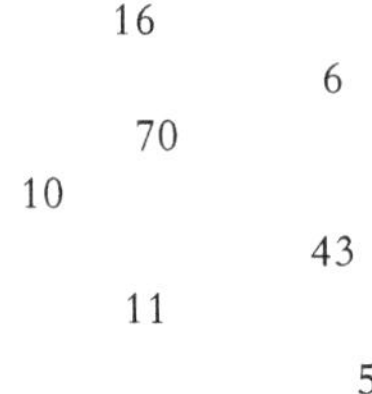

years old—straight people,
lifetimes painted by their numbers. Gay boys, only men for headlines, crime blotters, obituaries, while our Friday nights remain a viscous glass, a primo passed between acquaintances, a tipsy text message,
im somewhere iut jn Brioklyn with thia trick
Stolen manhood, in the thieving? Joyous, leaving nothing stuck to us but sweat, and nothing to our sweat but fast love, lifted weights, and pulses raced with party dust, a bedroom scandalous, luxurious with faggotry, and faggotry, a timelessness.

My friends, I pray if nothing else, delight in this:
our seeming agelessness, continuous—
an endlessness on end, and if someday it ends us,
then—

RESET

May 2001

This time,
when the captain of the swim team
comes back to his bedroom, damp
with shower water, boxers thin and
clinging to his legs, I do not freeze.

Instead, I drop fast to my knees and
throw my arms around
                    his slender waist.
I taste the warmth of him entire, and
we make love for the first time, both
of us, and to each other, on the floor
beside a moonlit wall of windows.

This time, we collapse
in mottled wreck of sweat, a skyline
ravaged by disaster,
    scraping from the rubble
            dazed and dirty,
                grateful and alive—

and this time,
        I don't fall for him, the redhead
from the trailer park who leaves me,
and I don't fall for my best friend
when he says he'll leave his lover for
me, and I don't fall for the boy with
black frame glasses who will teach me
how to need the heat of shame like
ugly drug until I only want to fuck
when certain I have been deceived.

I never kiss the actor backstage
in his black tuxedo, never watch him
hold a female co-star in the same way
he holds me in darkness
                    of a parked car—

and I never leave the countryside.
I never leave the country.
Never meet the handsome junkie
who will ruin me with grief,
or any of my closest friends.

I never find a man or art to love
that doesn't love me back.

and this time, I don't wonder what
became of him, my pretty little fish.
I never stare at pictures
of his wedding ring, as if it were
a life-preserver saving him
from drowning, as I drowned, in this,
the ugliest of all worlds.

I won't spend whole nights
remembering the details
of his teenage body, luminous
and almost-naked,
wet beside me in
his bed.

I'll never dream the life
I could have had, what it could have
been like, if I had known
if I had known

if

FREE LIVE CAMS

That it is *real*, is happening *right now*—
does nothing for me.
Still I'm curious enough to watch him,
thick Montana farmhand, handsome,
working himself over for small change.

He doesn't talk, but when there's
a request inside the chat— *Show hole!*
somebody says,
Lick your own feet!
a bell rings in acknowledgement
the payment's been received, and then
he apes amazement as if he were saying,

Me?

Do…what?

My…hole?

My feet?

At first it's irresistible, and then
repetitive, until at last like everything,
embarrassing.
A nuisance.
It is like the difference
between when Andy wouldn't kiss me,
and when Andy wouldn't kiss me
the third time.
A flashy paint, the straight man's shame.
A cock blushed hot rod, throbbing, each
unreachable, unwrangled, unforgettable
disaster of the senses—
then the fuel runs dry.

It used to be so genius.
All the bruises his not touching me
would leave behind.

CLEAN

Three days since I left him in the bed where later they would find him, cold—I wake up underneath a blanket, rattling inside myself. I stand but do not rise. It's funny how the phones keep charging. Everyone awake, and shedding light. My friends sit up with me in shifts, polite. I know I'm sticky underneath my clothes. The glass door to the shower slides apart. I'm naked, suddenly, the faucet spitting hot and water at my ankles, pooling gray, the salt dissolving from my beard. The way a body breaks into another, bathing is a pleasure both familiar and unsettling. Three days, and I know I'm expected to emerge somehow, to wash him from me, scrub filth from my flesh, despite how much it feels like I'm erasing him, expected to attempt some prettiness, wield delicate, soft language about boys as if we tumble into bed with aimless beauty—

almond blossoms blurring on the rippled surface of a lake, the dainty, pinkened rot of highbrow smut. I say, *The last time we made love, a song,*
a white horse ridden through the surf
and all of Africa, an unmade bed.
Inside me, seed, he buried it—a gift,
a wealth, he opened me, I begged.
He split me gorgeous, flooded me—

In truth our sex, as with our lives, is complicated and laborious and dirty with mechanics. In our hotel room in Tangier, I tried topping him. I pushed his legs apart, two heavy doors, before he slammed them shut and said,

I'm not sure if I'm clean.

In retrospect, I guess it was a little coarse to offer him the douche, explaining how to empty himself with it.

Jesus, Sean. he said, *Stop talking.*

[Just a few months later I'll be at a party with a large group of my friends all drunk and mostly women, brandishing their body positivity like tarnished bugles, dishing sexual technique in brassy reverie, the horror stories striped with alcohol and gag reflex, fat asses crammed in small back seats, the war wound of a blood-stained couch, *Oh men, how frail they are*, one says, to hoots and clinking glasses. I will start to tell this story, how he made me feel repulsive just for breaking the illusion, how I'd snapped at him and said— *Sex isn't magic. Sex is work. It doesn't happen by itself; we make it happen.* It becomes clear quickly this is not the kind of story people tell in conversations like this after all. No one will look at me. I'll taper off and feel rejected and confused, then someone else will change the subject while I leave the room.]

He's dead now, and I'm in the shower for the first time in three days. Perhaps it is the thinking about all of this that's done it—more than warmth or wet, the lick of soap across my neck, a strange and sudden privacy. Blood finds my cock. The sad old dog lifts up its head and whines for touch. I run my tongue across my teeth.

Male sweat, blade-sharp, tobacco, cheap hashish. Morocco, with its frigid seas and yellow walls. I'm standing in the claw foot tub, my eyes shut tight beneath the stream, the flimsy curtain shifting to allow him after me, The gripping of his palms, my shoulders bruising as he pulls me towards him, pulls himself against my back, inside of me again.

Inside of me again, right now and here.

The magic I did not believe in, difficult and clean. My legs give out. The steam uncoils from my back. It's over. I am gasping on my hands and knees. I'm sobbing down the drain. I don't expect you to believe me, but it happened. He was here. Alive again.

I swear, I actually could feel him.

He was holding me.

MARK WARD

TAKE A PICTURE OF THE NIGHT

MARK WARD IS THE AUTHOR OF *NIGHTLIGHT* **(SALMON POETRY, 2023) AND SIX CHAPBOOKS, THE MOST RECENT OF WHICH IS** *MASTERS* **(THE EMMA PRESS, 2025), A PAMPHLET OF RESPONSE POEMS TO DEAD QUEER MALE ARTISTS' WORK. A SECOND FULL-LENGTH COLLECTION,** *REAL ESTATE*, **IS FORTHCOMING FROM SALMON POETRY IN MAY 2026. HE IS CURRENTLY WORKING ON A VERSE NOVEL AND A THIRD COLLECTION.**

FRIDAY

What was notable was that it was not.
Its ordinariness quite endearing.

The day before we'd talked it through by text.

I had spent a few years flaying the thought
of a latex-free fuck to shreds. Despite

the PrEP, getting tested, I'd grown up with

tombstones falling: *Don't Die of Ignorance.*
A hushed monochrome burial foretold.

But I didn't die. And I needed to

know the difference. My asshole peeling
his foreskin back. His warmth leaking from me,

an indelible trail, the poet says

but after I wiped myself down and had
a shower, I felt exactly the same.

A NOTE TO MY BIOGRAPHER

Have you ever had frostbite?
A chill that won't leave your body
alone? That's poetry right there.
Fuck. These clumsy fingers,
I mostly got it on myself.
Another? No? I don't think
my life is interesting enough for
a throughline you can't embellish.
Reliant on mere facts,
everything becomes overshadowed
by them. A spider graph
demanding connections. I'm drunk.
At least that's what it feels like.
This medication. You're handsome,
the world will love that. Write
the best story you can but don't
pretend to know what I felt.

ICE CREAM IN THE SUN

That third drink was an unwinding,
a long slow exhalation.
You are little beyond a smile
and intent.

Spread across my face,
you drip, impossible to catch or keep
whole. The glut of bodies around us
swallows you.

Draped across the bar.
My mother would spit on a napkin
and clean my face if she saw me.
Your stickiness remains.

The next drink swings me
by both arms. A leer sidles up,
grabs my crotch, tests its weight.
I push him away.

Sobered up, I wash
my hands, face. I forget him, you,
find my friends. We call this place
home, unironically.

Nights here
aren't always the best but they're
ours. We dance. Is that you across
the bar?

I weave through the wall
of men, see you laughing, are you
waiting for me, were we a moment
or a start?

The leer grabs me,
squeezes, like you would a fruit.
The music blaring, I scream into
his ear.

He leers until I instruct security
to grab him by the scruff of
his neck, throw him out, him
flying high over all our heads.

The leer lands on the road and turns
to us as if to camera, eyes bulging
in surprise, still optimistic for
friendship.

I need a drink.
I try looking through the walls
of dancing flesh but they are
knitted tight.

I wash my hands,
face. The writhing bodies sweat.
I am freezing. I am a cool breeze
blown on freshly cooked chicken.

APATHY

The funhouse glittering
with menace. Its mirrors reflect
his insistence that you
enjoy this trip. His grin repeats

in every mirror.
He says that this was your idea
and you are surrounded
by a chorus of resentment.

And suddenly he's gone.
You walk into the wall and turn
smack into another,
terrified that there's no way out.

You feel for the exit,
wandering through a carnival
of other yous: starving,
bloated, shrunken, rail-thin

and not recognising yourself,
you start to run, shouting for him,
full of all those feelings
he asked of you. *Did you have fun?*

PASS

Better looking in person, I'm surprised
how nice it is to kiss him: soft, shallow,

frequent. His mountainous shoulders. I didn't
realise the quality of attention I wanted

that day: a look of quiet amazement,
his body latched to mine. I so easily forget

their names. He did everything right but
still, I find myself on the dual carriageway

unable to get a taxi, wishing for
something that was never on offer.

Longing is that distant threat, hovering
and this afternoon is a stopped clock. I walk

its absent time, tiptoeing along the big hand,
until, juddering back in sync, it throws me off.

TO THE MEN WHO LAUGHED WHEN I ASKED THEM IF THEY WERE ON PREP

Where do you get all your confidence from?
Muted light bleeding around the black tarp?
All those eager men buzzing around you?
That everyone is now within your grasp?

Or seems to be. You cannot abide this
stalling of your hard dick from what it needs.
That I must be an idiot to ask,
to assume that you would tell me the truth.

This isn't his soft confident chuckle,
a pair of safe hands resting on my shoulders.
It's your bitter laugh, your walking away.

To bring the world into this, when you want
holes and grunts. You return. I ask. Frustrated,
you spit out a *Yes* and screw your eyes shut.

LAST SUNDAY

He opens one eye to gauge the sunlight:
unobtrusive. The blankets coddle him.
He looks at the stone wall, the repetitive
greenery daubed everywhere,
settles on the overcast sky.

He decides to leave the other eye
closed, feeling more honest that way.
He makes a slight noise, a broken
humming in his throat to check that
he can still hear, and it fills him.

Sunlight quietly conquers his room.
He stares at its approaching shape,
closes his eyes. He focuses on the lights
duplicated in the darkness—stars, really—
filling the night sky of his eyelids.

The auroras slowly morph,
independent of him and the body
he no longer inhabits, until each
dissolves and he's left with the dark.
He keeps his eyes firmly shut, waiting.

SITUATIONSHIP

The thought of actually dating me
angers you. All your freedoms would wilt with
expectation. Better to sit in this
bluntness, front it out, call yourself toxic
proudly, and then pull me close, falling asleep
with your limbs wrapped around me, your heat
blanketing me. A magic trick, really,
how you say it means nothing but you fall

asleep in my arms, the first man to dream
in my bed beside me. How in a moment's
silence, you accuse me of just wanting
sex. It's all you can let yourself have,
the world won't disappoint you again. At dawn,
you complain about my snoring and head home.

★

When did these syllables become a rant?
No one likes to be disappointed but
think of the universe you're constructing.
Where are the poems about your happiness,
falling asleep in someone's arms, his texts
peppering a winter's day, sharing some
drunken chips? It wasn't love, you knew then,
a liberating clarity in this

growing closeness, an ease
there until it wasn't. I can't change it
but it doesn't have to be a cri de coeur.
Sometimes, a sunset watched through the glass doors
at your sister's place is just as worthy
of being in a poem, perhaps more so.

★

That night, for the first time since we started
talking again, you messaged me, and we shared
a naggin, news unfurling, life's irritants
held up to the light, examined and dropped.
An easy draping against each other.
You play with my hair. I say how nice it is
to be silent with someone. You murmur.
It is a long time before I lead you

to the bedroom. The animals in us
rut but we never lose sight of each other:
your hair, mussed and comical, as you
cum, face slack, dumb, adorable; your hand
adept at a rough tenderness, and after,
your arm rooting me to you through formless night.

⋆

I see you, housebound, all your curtains cut
down, sat by the window like a damned cat,
irritated by the slightest movements:
wind (always, wind) buffeting the branches,
a car chasing its licence plate, the moon
inching across an uninterested sky,
a man—you wonder if it's me—who doesn't
look up. You take a picture of the night

and post it. When I ask how you're doing
cooped up there, all you can imagine is misery,
me hobbling around my apartment
as your claws pick through what wasn't
love. Your silence would be fine if I didn't think
it was you slow-walking by my window.

⋆

And now, writing this, I'm struggling on
crutches. How exactly did you do this?
A hair woven into a voodoo doll?
A chipping away of my heel at night
until my calf collapses with the strain?
A soft curse spoken into the world?

But you swore you were above all that,
a better man than I—insensitive,
cruel—you insist you never think of me
yet your tiny avatar manifests
in seconds when I post a story. You
are fading silence, gas filling the room.
There was something true underneath these lines
but now all we are is a nod, hurt, this.

COMMANDMENTS FROM THE NEW LIFE

The oak continues to push itself
incrementally into the blue sky.

Morning never fails to show up,
unjudgmental, knowingly silent.

My father turns 88 and I watch
the odometer threatening reset.

The superking bed dwarfs me so I fill it
with men, with books like I did before.

Cobalt's love is boundless, resolute;
his excited tail wags so fast it blurs.

You talk about moving to the country
and you are still the you in my poems.

Often, the nights seem endless.
Somehow I never get enough sleep.

The oak flowers. Morning keeps watch.
Weeks, months pass. The world persists.

That line from *Blue Boy* echoing through:
'this new life no longer temporary'.

BUT THE NIGHTS

With every day I am more myself.
Conversation is a conscious choice
and I lean into phone calls:
their precarity, the static interruptions.
The kitchen stinks of bean juice and sweetcorn water
drained down the sink, a cupboard emptied.
You must accept that most times you won't get an answer
which is an answer, as the headless torsos insist.

Being alone changes you.
You wait until night is thick and walk in its quiet.
A small sneeze of rain announces itself.
With every day I am more myself.
I don't think I can ever recover.
My house, stinking of bleach, shining, waits for me.

JEFF WALT & HIS
DESERT RATS

THE DESERT RAT RESIDENCY FOR WRITERS IN PALM DESERT, CALIFORNIA, IS A RESORT-STYLE PRIVATE RESIDENCY OFFERING WEEKLONG RETREATS FOR WRITERS, WITH SPECIFIC RESOURCES AND AWARDS SET ASIDE FOR LGBTQ+ WRITERS. WRITERS CAN SIT BY THE POOL AND WORK ON NEW POEMS, START A NEW CHAPTER, CONSTRUCT A MANUSCRIPT, OR REVISE WORK. ALL WEEKLY RESIDENTS ARRIVE ON A FRIDAY AND DEPART THE FOLLOWING SATURDAY. AS OF 2024, 95% OUR VISITING WRITERS ARE CULLED FROM OUR ANNUAL CONTEST, *THE DESERT RAT POETRY & FICTION PRIZE*, **TO PROVIDE WRITERS WITH HOUSING & MEALS FOR SEVEN DAYS WHILE THEY WORK ON A WRITING PROJECT AND EXPLORE COACHELLA VALLEY. PARTNERS AND SPOUSES ARE WELCOME TO ATTEND THE RETREAT ALONGSIDE THEIR WRITERS.**

THE POETS IN THIS SECTION ARE MADE UP OF WRITERS WHO HAVE BEEN "DESERT RATS," AND MANY OF THE POEMS WERE WRITTEN DURING THEIR RESIDENCIES.

FOR MORE INFORMATION, PLEASE VISIT *WWW.DESERTRATRESIDENCY.COM*.

Stephen S. Mills is a Lambda Award–winning poet and playwright. His books include *He Do the Gay Man in Different Voices*, and his forthcoming poetry collection *Final Slash Boy* will be published by Broken Sleep Books. He lives in New York City.

Abby E. Murray is the editor of *Collateral* and the author of two poetry collections: *Hail and Farewell* and *Recovery Commands*. They live in the Pacific Northwest.

C. Dale Young is the author of a novel and six collections of poetry, the most recent being *Building the Perfect Animal: New and Selected Poems*. He lives in San Francisco.

S.A. Borland edits and designs at Sibling Rivalry Press and wrote *Tertulia*, a chapbook that gathers the dead and the living, the sacred and the domestic, into one room. saborland.com

Kelli Russell Agodon is a bi/queer poet from the Pacific Northwest and cofounded Two Sylvias Press. Her next book, *Accidental Devotions*, will be published by Copper Canyon Press in 2026. www.agodon.com

José Enrique Medina is the author of *Haunt Me* (2025 Rattle Chapbook Prize). His work appears in *Redivider*, *Best Microfiction 2019*, and *USA Today Hispanic Living*. You can find more of José here: IG @MedinaWrites | MedinaWrites.com

Michael Montlack's third poetry collection, *COSMIC IDIOT*, will be published by Saturnalia. He is the editor of the Lambda Finalist essay anthology *My Diva: 65 Gay Men on the Women Who Inspire Them* (University of Wisconsin Press). He lives in NYC and teaches poetry workshops at NYU and CUNY City College.

Steven Cordova's full-length collection of poetry, *Long Distance*, was published by Bilingual Review Press in 2010. From San Antonio, Texas, he lives in Brooklyn.

Jeannine Hall Gailey is a writer with MS who served as 2nd Poet Laureate of Redmond, Washington. She's the author of six books of poetry; her latest, *Flare, Corona*, from BOA Editions, was a finalist for the Washington State Book Prize. For more visit www.webbish6.com or Instagram @webbish6.

Ed Madden is the author of six books of poetry, most recently *A Pooka in Arkansas*, selected for the Hilary Tham Capital Collection.

Jeff Walt is Founder & Director of The Desert Rat Residency in Palm Desert, California, which he started to help other writers realize their aspirations via The Desert Rat Poetry & Fiction Prize with submissions open annually during the months of July & August.

WWW.DESERTRATRESIDENCY.COM

STEPHEN S. MILLS

IN LIFE I THINK OF THE RADIO COMMERCIAL FOR BURIAL PLANS I HEARD WHILE DRIVING IN PALM SPRINGS

as in *get it done now*
you might not have time later
as in *you don't want to be a burden to your family*
so pick a plot—a spot—pay for it now
who knows what might happen
all said in a cheerful radio-announcer voice
which makes me think of childhood summers
by the pool with my sister
listening to our favorite radio station
full of promises for all the things
coming this summer
followed by our favorite song: a distraction
but I'm 40 now
and the radio is reminding me of death—
my own death—of burial plans and plots and expenses
because death is expensive
as in death is a business
as in one of my favorite TV shows is *Six Feet Under*
set here in California in a funeral home
as in I saw Michael C. Hall on the subway platform
back home in New York
a few years ago
as in I've had my own obsession with death
nearly all my life
as in I find myself drawn to cemeteries
everywhere I visit:
Havana, London, Paris, L.A.
and now here in Palm Springs
as in I visit Desert Park Memorial
looking for Frank Sinatra
as in his grave
not the actual man
as in the man I most associate with New York
like that guy at the Yankees game
who used Old Blue Eyes to help insult another team

shouting: *We've got fucking Frank Sinatra, what do you have?*
as in Sinatra's "New York, New York" plays
after every single home game
no matter who wins
because even if we lose
we are still fucking New York City
and we are losing a lot right now
but this isn't New York
as in this cemetery is very flat
as in not very beautiful
on a scale of cemeteries I've visited
this might be the worst
as in Google Maps is bad at directing
you to small plots of land
as in I stumble around in 110-degree heat
searching
walking
back and forth
and back and forth
over flat grave markers
that you can't see
until you are on top of them
as in Google keeps telling me I'm there
right on top of Frank
but I'm not
I'm really not
and then suddenly I am
right over him
but now I'm overheated
and want to leave
so I snap a quick pic
and move to the shade of a lonely tree
as in I'm the only one here
as in it's too hot to be in a cemetery
looking for dead Hollywood
it is July in Palm Springs
but I am here
doing it my way
without a burial plot or plan
of my own.

ABBY E. MURRAY

ODE TO A CACTUS

Because I love a plant I can aspire to, flower
that will teach me to survive before it tells me
to be plentiful, that blooms when it feels like it

and never when it's told, and because it would sooner
impale the soft pad of your fingertip than dance
like an orchid or beg like a rose, and because

the cactus is a fist of knives to humans
but to the harmless elf owl it is home, and because
it casts no spell and says no prayer but sips

a hallowed water from the cup of no rain, and because
it thrives in the company of the forgetful and the hopeless,
because it is known to heal in the hands of women

and it bears a stubborn fruit—I give the cactus
my affection in a world of grasping stems
and clingy ruffles, a catalog of perfumes to delight me

and tender petals to sap my attention and hope
and worry and time, and because it is late in the day
and my head hurts and neither fragility nor elegance

can show me how to last in an environment
that would like to dry me out, starting with my liquid heart,
and because I will give the cactus all the nothing

it wants from me in exchange for lessons
on how to make my body a fence around what is unyielding
in its goodness, which can always be found in a desert.

C. DALE YOUNG

THE LAW OF DISPLACEMENT

Mild for the desert, the early morning
temperature is bearable enough to allow
one to stand by the pool drinking coffee.

Even this act is solitary and welcome,
the air barely stirring, the water's surface
unmoved and unmoving, perfectly still.

Archimedes was no Desert Father, but I
imagine him thinking deeply in the way
they did, looking and looking until what

cannot be seen is suddenly seen. Archimedes
would invite me to submerge myself
in the pool, the water displaced giving him

the volume of my body. I imagine Archimedes
as a Daddy telling me to be a good boy
and get into the pool, get wet for him.

The desert calls up so many odd scenarios.
I say "I am leaving you today," and the desert
sighs. One can imagine it rolling its eyes.

You see, you never really leave the desert
once you have spent more than a few days
in it. It changes your mind, changes your

physiology. It does not just take. Every thought
and every breath is now changed. The desert says:
Relax, I am inside you; I'm always with you.

S.A. BORLAND

THE RESORT

Someone at the entrance says,
Here to take a load off,
or here to take loads?

He sells shirts and condoms,
rhino pills and Gun Oil.
The price of what we hope for,
some brief heaven
made between bodies.

In the desert
people buy golf clubs,
join country clubs.
Or they come here,
chasing shade around the pool,
finding strangers in dark rooms,
where voyeurs cleave to the walls
like yucca blooming bayonets from stone.

It's my first time.
I'm still the southern boy,
minding shadows,
watchful of the shame
preached down my throat,
the boy who once spoke in tongues
and now uses mine
on a man.

I find sanctuary,
my head and nerves
hidden behind a paperback
I never meant to read,
watching everyone watching me,

shy as a hymn
and hungry for the solo.

At the pool, a bear pours airport bottles
of Jack over Fresca and ice.
I watch him strip, his shoulders wide as a pew,
his feet burning on the concrete.
The wanting runs up my throat
when he disappears
into the back rooms.

This voice in my ear:
There's a poem waiting for you back there.

Lit in the dark room
in the blue light of a shared fantasy
isn't the face I came for,
but a group defined by hunger.
One becomes that voice again:
Let me take care of you.

Later, a friend says,
His kink is nurturing.

In the dress shop
I was a boy running hands through silk,
careful, as if it might vanish.
The fabric felt like water
spilling through my fingers.

I let him inside me.
He asked what I wanted.
I said more.
He gave me more.
They circled me,
silent but for porn,
for thrusting.

When they touched me
I was the water
these men
slipped through.

I lost count.

I am always in control
or desperate to lose it.
Here I was both.
Saying, getting
what I wanted.

I was used, yes,
but used like a queen.
The hive alive,
sweet and stinging with honey.

Even then, I remembered
the back of the pew
holding me up, the hands
vibrating my throat, the hands
laid on my forehead,
the slick of the oil, some language
spilling from me like bees pouring from a wall,
a language for everything I thought
I could never have—
and yet it comes,
shimmering,
into me.

KELLI RUSSELL AGODON

WATCHING *THE DEVIL WEARS PRADA* IN PALM DESERT

On the cover of Vogue, a cactus, hints
of bougainvillea—*Florals for spring?*
How groundbreaking. The pool is a perfect
Tiffany blue. In the bathroom, Chanel No. 5
near the sink. If the devil wears Prada, the poet
wears flip-flops, a rainbow bikini. We debate
if tie-dye is in or out. *No. No.*
That wasn't a question. We are drinking on the patio
at prosecco o'clock. We say how the devil wasn't
Miranda Priestly but Andi's friends. We clink
our glasses understanding the true villain
is the boyfriend. A little tipsy, we google
"white Prada loafers." You ask me if I could be
the devil. I say—*Only if I have the right shoes.*

JOSÉ ENRIQUE MEDINA

MEN SEEKING MEN: PERSONAL ADS

1. AM I ASKING FOR TOO MUCH?

Mind reader wanted.
You'll predict my needs before I speak them.
You'll be trauma-free, debt-free, and full of surprises.

Me: high-functioning control freak
with Louis Vuitton emotional baggage and a weak spot for
programmable robots.

Applicants must be blank slates
eager to be rewritten.
If you've ever rebooted your soul, we might be compatible.
Upgrades encouraged. No messy backstories.

2. PARTY TIME

Hi. I'm charming. Addictive. A total nightmare.

Looking for someone with soft eyes, a soft job, and a soft spine.
If you earn enough, you won't notice when I blow it on booze.

When I'm angry, I won't punch—
I'll hold you down just enough to remind you
I could.

Bonus points if the smell of weed and gym socks turns you on.
If I threaten to jump off a roof,
you'll just know I need a hug.

3. COMMITMENT

ISO partner to cheat on, regularly.

You'll find texts. I'll lie.
You'll cry. I'll say, "You're right. I'm sorry."
And you'll forgive me.
We'll hold each other tighter
like people who know this is doomed.

I'm fair—
you can cheat too. Just don't be obvious.
Let's destroy each other sweetly,
while sipping turmeric lattes and planning our wedding.

Monogamish. But mostly not.

4. CONFIDENT & MATURE

Me: 42, emotionally asthmatic.
You: 60s, stylish, unattached, perfect on paper, terrified of real closeness.

Let's meet. Pretend we're versions of ourselves we admire.
Let's charm each other into thinking this might work.

Later, when you flirt with the bartender,
I'll smile like it doesn't gut me.
I'll excuse myself with grace,
touch both your elbows gently,
and say, "I'll leave you two to talk."

Your line is:
"No. Don't go."
Say it. Please. Say it like you mean it.

So I can walk away anyway
and replay the scene
for the rest of my life.

MICHAEL MONTLACK

THE 80S WERE SOOO GAY

Not that we knew it, spinning
around the junior high dance to
"Do You Really Want to Hurt Me,"
shrugging off perplexed parents
when they asked if Boy George
was really a boy. *Um, we dunno.*
We just loved the song.

We were busy anyway, spritzing
our hair to Heavy Metal heights—
head-banging to Twisted Sister's
Dee Snider at the mic in hulking
Goldilocks drag—pausing maybe
to fully absorb the *Like-a-Virgin*
Madonna humping the stage
in a mini bridal dress on MTV
or to scour the mall for leather
shops that sold wrist cuffs like
dom Rob Halford's of Judas Priest.

We were clueless in the deluge.

Dynasty, *Golden Girls*, Pee-wee
Herman, Tammy Faye—hell...
wasn't Rubik's Cube, when jumbled,
like a Cyndi Lauper "wainbow?"

Even the most homophobic jocks
belted "We Are the Champions" naked
together in locker room showers,
sporting their Mercurial mustaches—
the innuendo of *Queen* lost on them,
not unlike Reagan's oblivion to AIDS.

STEVEN CORDOVA

POETRY IN MOTION

I stop to read
a Toi Derricotte poem.

It appears
propped

on a bed of pixels
only to disappear

before I've managed to read
the last line

& is oh-so-rudely replaced
by an advertisement!—

for razor blades!
I move on,

stop to read
a Victoria Chang poem

& it too disappears!—
this time

before I've managed to read
the first line!

Meanwhile I miss my train!—
& the handsome passenger who cruised me!

Some days are like that.
Poetry just escapes you.

JEANNINE HALL GAILEY

WHEN YOU SAID "PALM SPRINGS" I HEARD PSALM SPRINGS

for Jeff Walt

which sounds very spiritual,
although I know the trippy steakhouse-martini-spa-kitsch
ode to the desert doesn't inspire sacred thoughts,
no Sunday School hymnbooks haunted by Sinatra.

But wait, maybe the whole city is a kind of psalm—
a praise to late night neon, strong cocktails, chemical water?
Isn't there graffiti of rainbow wings about to lift us up
called "Stay Human" as if we are all about to take flight,

transform into brightly colored street angels?
Anyway, it is an oasis, acres of dates and grapefruit,
lemons and olives on the trees, wildflowers
blooming in the sand after a midwinter deluge.

Isn't that what we're all searching for?
I think of Jesus in the desert, tempted by Satan—
did he ever even imagine a desert like this,
slightly seedy, slightly swaggering, like the drunk

businessman who tried to get your number
or the check-in clerk who slipped you his,
like the hummingbirds buzzing around flowers
in February? What God refuses a psalm

built from the will to live in hard places
between sand and mountain, full of hidden
miracles, hot springs and shimmering graffiti wings?

ED MADDEN

NORTH

"We have both sides here to talk with everyone."

- Sept 18, 2024

The tattoo artist lifted the north star
from the map on my back—more flower

than star—and put it on my left shoulder.
A way to get my bearings. As I sat there

in the quiet studio, end of the day, she filled in
the outline with orange and red, flesh and blood,

while a few blocks away a founder of the Proud Boys
told college girls the only way to get ahead

is by giving head and offered two of them fifty
bucks to make out in front of the rowdy crowd.

The other speaker poured white goo from a bucket
labeled 'cum' on a college boy's head as he listed

all the faculty he intended to sue. The cum
was the cue for next slide of a faculty name

and face and sometimes phone number—a model
of civility and reasonable discourse and the thoughtful

consideration of alternate points of view
which helps us to arrive at the truth. He called

the professors pedophiles and rapists and carpet-munchers—
and said of one, 'she looks like a Jew.' This is what

counts as free speech these days. Only
a few blocks south, the university was serving hotdogs

to students avoiding the dining hall while white
nationalists filled the building. A few blocks north,

I was getting a star, a flower, a burning
symbol of direction carved into my shoulder,

as if to say, that which is beautiful is what
will guide me. This one didn't hurt at all,

my whole body buzzing with endorphins
and decision.

JEFF WALT

TAKE ME

Out here on the damp deck, bare feet, splintered wood,
smoke curling from my lips like a question I'm too tired to ask.

The stars hang like busted porch lights—some dead, some dying,
some still pretending they've got a job to do.

I ash into a beer can and tip my head back
until my neck aches. Just waiting.
For something.
For *someone*.

If I squint long enough, every blinking plane
becomes a promise.
Every satellite a possibility.

Neighbors are asleep—lives tucked in:
alarm clocks set, coffee makers ready
to brew another day they don't want.

Me?
I want out.
Not in a metaphor.
Not a fresh start or some "journey inward." I mean *gone*.

Lifted from the gravity
of rent, family group texts,
this body I keep
trying to forgive.

If they came—
silver ship,
soft hum—
I'd step in barefoot, no questions. No note
on the kitchen table. No forwarding address.

Let them probe me, wipe me clean. Make me a new thing,
or nothing at all.
Just don't leave me here.

A dog barks down the road.
The wind shifts.
Something rustles in the trees but stays hidden.

I light another smoke. Whisper into the dark,
Take me. Please. I won't fight.

And above,
the stars pulse like they're breathing
the way I'm breathing,
their burning like my burning.
Lightyears and yearning.

SARA YOUNGBLOOD GREGORY

GONE BUT NOT DEAD

SARA YOUNGBLOOD GREGORY IS AN AWARD-WINNING LESBIAN JOURNALIST, EDITOR, AND AUTHOR. HER WORK HAS BEEN FEATURED IN *THE NEW YORK TIMES*, *THE NEW REPUBLIC*, *NEW YORK MAGAZINE*, *VICE*, *TEEN VOGUE*, *COSMOPOLITAN*, *THE GUARDIAN*, *THEM.US*, **AND ELSEWHERE. SARA SERVES ON THE BOARD OF THE LESBIAN LITERARY AND ARTS JOURNAL** *SINISTER WISDOM*, **WHERE SHE IS CURRENTLY EDITING THE FORTHCOMING BUTCH-FEMME RENAISSANCE ISSUE. SHE WAS THE NEWS AND REPORTING SPRING 2023 FELLOW AT TRANSLASH MEDIA, COVERING ANTI-TRANS LEGISLATION AND COMMUNITY ORGANIZING IN HER HOME STATE OF FLORIDA. IN 2023, SARA WAS THE RECIPIENT OF THE CURVE AND NLGJA AWARD FOR EMERGING JOURNALISTS. THE SAME YEAR, HER SPECULATIVE POETRY COLLECTION** *DEAD BOYS IN SPACE* **WON THE 2023 PAMET RIVER PRIZE FROM YESYES BOOKS AND WILL BE PUBLISHED IN MAY 2026.**

ON SCI-FI, SPECULATIVE POETRY, AND THE AIDS CRISIS

As a child, there were only two things I knew about my cousin: he was gay, and he died of AIDS.

I could tell you more things, now. He was an artist. He went to college. I know he liked to make women laugh, eat fancy cheeses, and bring gorgeous, flamboyant lovers home for holidays. I know he lived in New York City. I know it took a long time for him to die. So long that he had the time to nurse and bury two boyfriends and a roommate, and maybe others my mother didn't know about or just didn't have the heart to mention. When he got sick, I know he went to Lennox Hill and when he got so, so sick he went back home to New Jersey. I know that, at the end, he was in so much pain he couldn't bear to be touched. I know that he was 32.

Growing up, my cousin was a ghost, the outline of which any child could feel but knew not to ask about. When I came out at 18, I still didn't ask. But I did grieve. I began to understand, for the first time, the enormity of what I had lost: a mentor, a friend, a teacher, a bad influence, an example, a road map, a dream, a cousin, a brother. One day it occurred to me I may have also lost a rival or a bully. Someone whom I hated, and who hated me back. How gratefully I would have accepted *any* relationship with him, even a difficult one.

My coming out was painful for my family. I still sometimes wonder if his life—or more accurately the tragedy of his death—was the stick by which my own homosexuality was measured. Or if not the stick, then the poisoned well from which I drew. Without him, I was the only one in our family. I felt like an alien; I had to make contact.

So I started writing not *to* my cousin, but *towards* him. On the page, I could ask anything I needed to know. There was no one to say the grief wasn't mine, or that the government didn't murder him, or that because I didn't know him, I couldn't claim him. I claimed him. On the page, he was dead, but he didn't have to be gone.

After a while, I began asking the opposite, twin question: what if he was gone, but he didn't have to be dead?

In my poetry collection *DEAD BOYS IN SPACE*, I imagine a world in which a generation of gay men did not die from AIDS. That's not to say I imagined a world in which the government responded appropriately or where middle America suddenly cared deeply for the health and happiness of people with HIV/AIDS. That world that still does not exist. Instead, I asked: What if the United States government got its wish? What if they really *could* disappear thousands and thousands of sick men? And what if that place was the moon? And my biggest leap—what if their exile was actually a blessing, a literal coup against death? The ultimate otherness and a final liberation, as Jon Greenberg wrote for the political funeral of his friend and fellow AIDS activist Mark Lowe Fisher?

DEAD BOYS IN SPACE isn't autobiographical or memoir. It is science fiction as much as it is poetry, with invented characters and situations. On the page, I didn't create a relationship with my cousin. But I did create a world in which a relationship was possible—for me and everyone else touched by this generational grief.

I am 29 now, newly and unexpectedly living in New York City. I imagine us walking the same streets, looking at the same river, maybe going to the same bars. If he were still alive, my cousin would be 61 years old. I am fairly certain he died the same year I was born—1996. The synchronicity sometimes scares me. But I tell myself it was meant to be that way, that we are locked in opposite, but twin, orbits. That it must have happened but I just can't remember it—us, together. Making contact. Him, just freshly in death. And me, in utero, not quite in life. The same plane of existence. Not touching. Not speaking. But, for a moment, waving from a great distance. Like the moon and the tides.

Book Title: *DEAD BOYS IN SPACE*
Publisher: YesYes Books
Publication Date: May 19, 2026
Publisher Website: www.yesyesbooks.com
Author Website: saragregory.org

YOU WANNA BE IN ASSARACUS?

JUST EMAIL ME.
TELL ME WHY.

bryan@siblingrivalrypress.com

I'LL DO MY BEST TO MAKE A DIVERSE, FUN, SEXY, SACRED PLACE FOR QUEER POETRY.

save lives save lives save lives save lives

I ESPECIALLY LOVE PUBLISHING QUEER ELDERS AND NEVER-BEEN-PUBLISHED-BEFORE POETS.

you belong you belong you belong you belong

REVIEW IDEAS?
FORTHCOMING TITLES?
INTERVIEW IDEAS?
PITCH ME. WANNA DANCE?
LET'S DANCE.

BRYAN'S POEM

MUSHROOMS

Jason Schneiderman left a chocolate bar with psychedelic mushrooms at Desert Rat with Jeff Walt. Or he turned Jeff on to mushroom-infused chocolate bars, and either way, with Jason to thank, Jeff gave us a full bar, 18 squares with guidance for dosage. 1-2 microdosing, 3-4 therapeutic, and anything beyond that turns you into a god. I live my life with one foot in the spirit world. I met my first ghost when I was young enough to take an afternoon nap in my grandmother's bed: a dog that had died the week before. He was loving. He was checking on me. This was in the same house, around the same time that I saw a man in the mirror watching me. I wasn't afraid. I was *interested*. All this saying it doesn't take much for me to dance through the veil. I went with 3 squares of chocolate, being a lightweight in everything from gin to poppers to marijuana, having once been high for several days off an edible from Megan Volpert I ate at a writing conference on an empty stomach. I levitated. My body turned into a bobsled. I bobsledded into the bathroom, which became a spacecraft of some sort. Everything was a vehicle I recklessly drove. Across the room, Megan slept. She was decidedly *not* a lightweight.

What I can report: Seth and I swam and were amused by our shadows in the water. They didn't seem to be attached in any way to our bodies or our movements.

We listened to the demo of "Girls Just Wanna Have Fun" when it was more punk in style. Holy shit.

Seth fucked me in several positions for the duration of an entire Blood Orange album. More than a vehicle, I became a portal.

I didn't see a god or the cosmos. There was no other man in the mirror. I saw my own face, repeatedly, even when I was not looking.

What do you think that means?

www.ingramcontent.com/pod-product-compliance
Lightning Source LLC
LaVergne TN
LVHW052341100826
845147LV00021B/1147

9781943977956